The Diary of a
Rum-Runner

THE SUPERCARGO

The Diary of a Rum-Runner

BY ALASTAIR MORAY

FLAT HAMMOCK PRESS
MYSTIC, CONNECTICUT

Flat Hammock Press
5 Church Street
Mystic, CT 06355
(860) 572-2722
www.flathammockpress.com

Originally published 1929, P. Allan & Co. Ltd.

Publisher's Preface, Publisher's Afterword © 2007 by Flat Hammock Press

Printed in the United States of America

10 9 8 7 6 5 4 3 2 1

ISBN10: 0-9773725-6-1
ISBN13: 978-0-9773725-6-0

CONTENTS

BOOK II

BOOK III

PUBLISHER'S PREFACE

PROHIBITION, which made the manufacture, sale, and transportation of intoxicating liquor illegal in the United States, became effective on January 16, 1920, through ratification of the 18th Amendment to the Constitution and passage of enforcement laws known as the Volstead Act. Instead of its desired effect of ridding American society of the detriments of alcohol, Prohibition actually increased the demand for whiskey, rum, and other hard liquor.

To satisfy this growing thirst, many enterprising Europeans seized the economic opportunity and began shipping liquor, first to islands like the Bahamas, and later, to avoid customs duties, directly to the waters off the major population centers of the U.S. Rum running, as it became known (rum being a term that came to embrace all sorts of liquor), was highly profitable, and the risks were low.

Scotsman Alastair Moray, like many in Great Britain (and all of Europe for that matter) who found themselves in the grips of a severe economic depression following the Great War, needed work. In the new rum running trade, the position of supercargo paid especially well. The supercargo—the term short for cargo superintendent—was the important individual who served as the owner's representative and who oversaw the cargo and handled the commercial transactions of the voyage.

By the time Alastair Moray—or whatever his actual name was—entered the rum running trade, the process was well established. The rum ships, flying the British or French ensigns for the most part, simply took station legally outside the U.S. three-mile (later 12 mile) limit of jurisdiction and waited for fast motorboats to come out, purchase a cargo, and rush it ashore past the Coast Guard patrol vessels. Whether it went to organized crime figures or thirsty community leaders made no difference to the supply ships. The Coast Guard would increasingly expand its efforts to suppress this trade, but it continued from 1920 through 1933.

The rum running described in this book was carried out from September 1923 through August 1924. Moray's diary for the 11 months is perhaps the most descriptive—and readable—account of daily life on Rum Row extant today.

INTRODUCTION

THERE was a day when I walked along near the Central Station, Glasgow. Having often done this before, I little suspected where this particular piece of pedestrianism would ultimately land me.

Halfway to my destination, Fate, in the shape of a 'pal,' stopped me, blinked solemnly at me through a pair of horn-rimmed glasses for a minute, and, to my surprise, said, "How would you like to go as supercargo in a rum runner?"

Whew! It rather took my breath away for a moment.

"Well," I said, "let's have some further particulars."

"Right," he said; "come up to an office here and I'll introduce you to the man who told me about it."

So we set off, and in the said office I was duly introduced to Mr. Cork, who proved a genial gentleman. Mr. Cork explained to me that he and another were arranging to send about 20,000 cases of the best out to the coast of America in a four-masted schooner owned by his friend, and that they required a supercargo. He explained that the voyage would start about the beginning of September, and that it was expected to take from three to four months. In fact, it was believed that three voyages would be made in a year.

"I'll tell you what," he said. "Think it over; go down and see the ship. The captain is on board; have a yarn with him, and let me know how you feel about it the day after tomorrow."

"All right," I said, and we left it at that. He told me the connections in New York had already been established, and he understood they were the best obtainable.

The next day I wandered down, and, after some trouble, located the ship, went on board, and asked a gentleman who was loafing about in his shirt-sleeves where I could find the captain. He replied, "I am the captain." So I informed him I might be coming with him on his next trip as supercargo. We shook hands, and he *said* he was glad to hear it. We had a chat and a smoke together, he telling me some yarns of the Magellan Straits in dirty weather, and other parts of the world; I perforce keeping silence, since my experience of the sea had been confined to a wee motorboat on the Clyde and a lug-sail in summer in the West Highlands.

I don't think, however, he was too enthusiastic over the sailing qualities of the *Cask*. However, by the time I had got back to the city I had made up my mind to go. I told Mr. Cork so the following day, and he informed me that the lad whose idea it was would be in his office the next forenoon and I had better turn up and meet him. This I did, and then and there it was settled.

Our cargo was to arrive next week, and that meant a queer lot to arrange and get done in the interval. Firstly, the matter of protection. I was informed that an unarmed ship out there was as safe as the proverbial snowflake, so, with the object of being safer than the snowflake, I purchased six .450 Webley revolvers, one Colt .45, an automatic .38, and plenty of ammunition. The boss, as we now called him, had a rifle, and a 'great secret' which I was to know about later on.

A safe was the next purchase. I wanted a good one, but was only allowed to spend £4 on it, so we took one aboard that a nigger baby could have opened blindfolded.

My next care was for our moments of relaxation. For these I bought a Wheatstone concertina which I knew nothing about. I added my bagpipes, which I knew a little about, and a small library, including Captain Lecky's *Wrinkles On Practical Navigation*; also a camera with a good supply of films.

On Monday, the 27th of August, the *Cask* was alongside the loading-sheds, and the first of the cargo was due alongside the following morning. So I was soon to be at my job of supercargoing, and, although ignorant, I trusted I would prove an adaptable bloke.

Loading, loading, loading, using all three hatches. It was a great game watching for theft. One brilliant soul was caught just in time as he wheeled a hand-cart containing eleven cases of White Horse out of the shed.

By the end of the first day a fair number of the loading-crew were very merry and bright. The idea is, when stowing a case, to land it hard down on its corner, which breaks a bottle; then, using a cap in lieu of a tumbler, to drink your own health or anybody's you like. By the evening of the 31st all was on board and the hatches on. All that remained was to wait till the next day, take the pilot to our bosoms, plant him on the bridge, and do as he directed until he decided we might be trusted not to interfere with the banks of the river, or other shipping who have as much right there as we have.

BOOK I

CHAPTER I

THE START

1st September.—We sail this morning. I got down to the *Cask* early, which was fortunate, for the cook came and asked where the officers' plates, knives, forks, tumblers, etc., were. Search showed that they weren't. That meant a wild rush to the nearest shop and the hasty purchase of all the needful articles for eight persons. Got back to the ship with two lassies staggering along after me with a large clothes-basket containing the mess equipment, to find the dock gate opening and a tug ambling in with an important air. All tugs are important (to tugs).

Our pilot is on the bridge. The friend who introduced me to the venture, looking quite like an excited 'Hoolet' with his horn-rimmed glasses on, and Mr. Cork arrive. We shake hands, and I go aboard. The boss arrives, goes on board, and we are ready. A whistle from the pilot. The tug starts. We follow because we can't help it, someone having connected us with a wire hawser. Never mind; we have a tilt at the quay wall on our way out of the narrow exit from the dock, just to let the tug see she can't have it all her own way, and we manage to dent the taffrail on the poop. Wave a last farewell to my two friends, who are standing at the exit from the dock and appear from their gesticulations to be having trouble with a large and offensively familiar plague of flies.

Our progress down the river was nothing if not pleasant and successful, after the pilot had told the skipper that he wouldn't go any further unless a sober man was put at the wheel. After some search, a gentleman answering to that description was found.

Stowed some coils of rope and barrels of salt horse in the

fore-hold. One dropped and smashed up a wooden cradle, but, as the boss was artistically driving No. 1 winch at the time, we smiled and said it didn't matter; nor did it, anyhow.

Spent some time adjusting compasses, of which we have three on board.

Our officious tug came alongside at Gourock and took off our passengers, plus pilot.

By the time we were off Wemyss Bay, our 250 h.p. engine was running strongly, and I took the opportunity to test our speed on the Skelmorlie mile. We were doing, I found, 5.47 knots per hour under engine only. The sails we shall leave for a day or so; in fact, till such time as our crew have forgotten there are such things as last days ashore.

They all turned up but the donkeyman, whom we shall need to seek in Havre. A beautiful night, and calm, with a good N.W. wind to blow us down towards the Isle of Man and the open sea.

2nd September.—A perfect day. Ambled quickly along, with our N.W. faithfully following. At 11 a.m. we got a jib and foresail on the foremast. Hard work hoisting the large foresail, as some of our crew are not yet available.

Got all my kit stowed; oiled up our sidearms and put them out of harm's way.

Wind veered round by S.E. to S.W. between 5 p.m. and 8 p.m. Air light, however. We are abreast of Dundalk at 7, and travelling about 7 knots. Ship slowly losing its Glasgow grime.

3rd September.—Beautiful morning. There is a member of this expedition who must be in introduced, and that is 'Ping Pong,' a native of China. He is a cheerful Oriental, can call up a smile at any moment, and is at present acting as assistant engineer. We get on well, I think. By the by, although, according to Clark Russell, Cutcliffe Hyne, and other writers of marine fiction, we ought to have discovered a stow-away about five days out, with the poor beggar in a state of exhaustion from starvation, we actually found ours the second day out. A careful search of the ship for a missing collar-stud brought to light the fact that we had two of these curious people on board, so we are ahead of fiction, anyhow. They are both young, one very young—I don't think he is over seventeen—and the other about twenty-three. They appear to be willing workers, and have been turned to at various jobs, so we shall probably sign them on the articles later. There are no bunks for them, so I don't know where they are dossing.

At eight bells this morning we were due east of the Sugar Loaf, abreast of Bray. About midday the glass started to back, and a bank of cloud came up from S.W. Wind freshening. By 5 p.m. we were making no headway; in fact, rather the reverse. The ship was rolling a good deal, and about a half gale was blowing. Put about, and hoisted trysail on jiggermast to steady her, as we were drifting too near the English coast.

It is 9 p.m., and at the moment we don't know exactly where we are, as we are still drifting more or less rapidly N., and nothing is visible to get a bearing on. Raining, and wind very fresh. Big sea running now. I am very much afraid this ship won't see the lights outside of New York for a considerable time. Our engines are not powerful enough; in fact, they can't give us steering way against even a moderate wind and sea.

It might be as well, at this point, to give a brief description of the swift saloon vessel I am in. She is a four-masted schooner built for the timber trade, and only has store accommodation for about eight to fourteen days out of port. The result is that, as we have six months' provisions on board, every available corner is littered with bags of coffee, beans, peas, lentils, etc. The bath aft is up to the brim with tins of Australian beef and mutton, and all the lockers in the small saloon are overflowing. Her registered tonnage is 390. She is 170 ft. between perpendiculars, 33 ft. beam, and at present draws 12 ft. 6 in. aft and 11ft. 6in. forward. She is flat-bottomed and has no keel, so her leeway is enormous—practically four points with a beam wind. I know that if you stand on the poop and look astern, her wake goes off nearly at right angles.

Her steel masts are fitted with patent runways for the sail cleats, which jamb at the slightest excuse. The mainboom and mizzen boom are about 10 ft. above the hatches, so that more wind goes underneath than is good for our progress. Her holds are splendid; in fact, the ship is one large hold. The only bulkheads are at the forepeak tank and the engineroom right aft, not counting temporary wooden ones between the three hatches.

She has three tanks in her double bottom, the largest containing forty-five tons of fresh water. The forepeak has nine tons; the other two tanks contain sixty tons of fuel oil. She has fine, high hatch-coamings. The jiggermast on the poop is also the engine exhaust. She. won't tack without the assistance of the engine, when there is a breeze worth speaking of, but just comes up almost into the wind and then falls off again. So, when we decide to go off on the other tack, we have to wear her round. She carries a donkey boiler on the starboard side amidships for windlass and winches. The port side is the mess-room and galley.

So much for introduction. She will doubtless exhibit other traits and peculiarities as the voyage progresses.

It has got worse. A nasty big sea is running now (time 10 p.m.), and things are moving that ought to stay still. About 10:30 p.m. we took in all canvas except the inner jib and trysail, as we were rolling so badly. The gaffs were lashing about and looked like carrying away, despite the gaff guys (which, however, are only single pur-chase). I'll need to chuck this till tomorrow, as the ship is jumping about too much.

CHAPTER II

THE *CASK* AT SEA

4th September.—It is daylight and the wind has changed. We had a great night. About eleven I got fed up trying to stand on my feet without putting a hand on the deck to steady myself, so went to my bunk, which is really the skipper's. Just through from my bunk, and divided from it by a wooden partition, is the pantry store. About 11:30 p.m. the roll got worse, and something started off on its own, something heavy that appeared to be trying to get through the wooden bulkhead at my head. In a minute or two there was a crash, and, says I to myself, says I, "Better see what's doing, young fellow-me-lad." Wandered out into the alleyway with my cold feet on the bare floor, and found that the pantry door had been carried away and the alleyway was full of prunes and raisins out of two cases that had charged the door and burst themselves with laughing at their success. Jammed the door shut and went back to my bunk. Walking on those currants was very like walking on black-beetles. After picking the currants from between my toes, I settled down, and was promptly ejected by a big roll.

There is a safe sitting on deck just above my room, and presently it started to slide, and brought up with the devil of a row, as though it had gone through the starboard lifeboat. The safe is in my department and should have been lashed, so *that* meant a journey on deck.

After some trouble I managed to get it lashed up against a bollard. Lashing a heavy safe on a pitch dark night in a gale of wind on a ship out of control is nearly as difficult as looking for a black cat in a dark room when the damn thing isn't there, and, to add to the hilarity of the moment, my pajama trousers were blown down half a dozen times. Got to sleep about 6:30 a.m., when the wind shifted into the north, and we got up the foresail and mainsail. The mate has a nice lump on his head through being landed on the floor out of his bunk. Nothing much happened during the day, except that at about eleven the mainsail split down the middle, and had to come down. Sighted the Smalls Light on our starboard bow when the naughty thing should have been to port. It has taken us all our time to round it as the wind has shifted back to the S.W. A good thing we did round it, as otherwise we would have had another night just messing about. We are now on our course to clear Land's End, which we should fetch about ten tomorrow night if the wind keeps as it is.

There appears to me to be a lot of uncertainty about this ship. Her gear aloft is not too good, and her machinery should be at least three times as powerful for this job. She was built in 1916, and nothing has been renewed since.

I noticed that the skipper's entry in the scrap log for last night was 'Ship out of control. drifting N.E.' I shall have to write from Havre to tell my Glasgow friends not to expect us off America for a bit longer than was reckoned.

I tried the concertina this afternoon, but can't make head or tail of the dashed thing.

5th September.—A splendid run today. Nothing has gone wrong. We had a fairly stiff breeze from the west, which shoved us along at about 6 knots, our average for the last seventeen hours. We nearly had an encounter with a large French fishing boat, which wouldn't get out of the way until the last moment. Our stem wasn't 20 ft. off her when she saw something she wanted to examine at a distance in another direction. I don't understand colloquial French, but what they appeared to shout was enough to blister the paint on the galley funnel. Shortly afterwards we passed a dredger being towed, and making very heavy weather of it. Rather uncomfortable, I should think, in a heavy sea.

Skipper was in great form today, and told several people that he knew all about their attainments and probable ancestry, in fact both probable and improbable. I am settling down to this life fine and am more than beginning to enjoy it. Had a long talk about the New York idea, and captain, who knows the place well, says it is going to be very difficult at this time of the year, in this ship, anchored in the open sea, with winter gales arriving with the full power of the Atlantic behind them. He thinks we should run down to the West Indies, and run the cargo in the early spring. That notion rather appeals to me, as I haven't seen the West Indies. However, I must obey orders, and we can't have expenses running on like that.

At present we are getting well up the Channel, and should be abreast of the Eddystone Light about midnight. Assisted the engineer for a bit while he put on a new fuel-pump spring.

6th September.—Nothing to say about today that is worth recording, except that this evening, about eight bells, saw a steamer approaching us. When we first saw her lights she would be a mile away. I think either her old man was drunk or asleep, or the quartermaster steering, was, for she showed us her port light six times before deciding what she would do. We kept our course east-sou'-east, and she passed us only thirty yards off.

A perfect day, with the wind aft, averaging about five knots. Passed the Casquets light at eight. Channel Islands are now behind, so we should be in Havre tomorrow about 11 a.m.

7th September.—We are splendid prophets on board. I prophesied that we should reach Havre about 11 a.m. Well, we eventually got in at 2:30 p.m., which was as near as prophets can expect to get in these days. Sighted Havre in the distance about 10 a.m., or, rather, we sighted a lightship which lies off about seven miles. Captain is in quite a genial humour, but rather worried at the non-appearance of the pilot, who should have met us well outside. He has been having great fun with a bucket of water on the bridge and has managed to get himself thoroughly shaved (his first since Glasgow), and I must say it has made him a changed man.

We picked up our pilot at last, and under his careful supervision we got safely alongside. I was almost sure there would be a catch somewhere about the pilot; he looked much too innocent. Well, he suddenly pounced on me, not, however, to give him his due, without an introduction. This was effected by the captain in true courtly style, by jerking his thumb at me and saying, "There he is; that's him in the dirty shirt; give them to him." All this merely meant the filling up of a sheaf of papers consisting of questions such as: 'Have you seen any rats?' If so, 'How many?' The French may be very polite, but I consider that the innuendo in these words, was entirely uncalled for, considering our cargo.

On arriving inside the breakwater we were proceeding peacefully to where the pilot thought we should go when a very excited gentleman waved an umbrella at us in a most aggressive way from the dock wall and ordered us to go in quite a different direction. This gentleman turned out to be the owner of the boat, so to please him we went over to where he directed. About three hours later, again just to please him, we started off for our original destination, with myself and a gentleman known as Martin (of whom more anon) at the wheel. Our destination was the far end of the system of docks, the approaches being canal-like with plenty of right-angle turns. The steering chains were very slack even with the adjusting rigging screws tight up, so, although we had two men at the wheel, it was quite hard work.

Having put on more decent garb, I went ashore, wandered to the hotel and had dinner with the boss, as he is called. A very pleasant meal, which I enjoyed the more for having already dined on board our floating hotel. Nearly lost myself on the way back, had an altercation with a gendarme at the dock gate, but got the better of the exchange of compliments, and reached the *Cask* at 12:30 a.m.

I have just realized why we have made for a continental port instead of going straight over. Apparently there is a Customs' drawback on all our cargo when the landing certificates are received back home. We are to discharge here so as to obtain the landing certificates, after which we put the stuff all back again and proceed where we like, as nothing further is necessary to obtain the *£. s. d.* back.

THE *CASK*

BENDING A NEW FORESAIL

CHAPTER III

AT HAVRE

8th September.—Up at 6:30 a.m. A day of toil and a deuce of a lot of running about. We started discharging from all three hatches at 7:30 a.m. About two hundred excited French men were responsible for getting the cargo out, and also responsible for getting some of it in (themselves). I think they were all in league against me, and in partnership to see just how much whisky they could manage to steal. One of the first to try was a gentleman in a skip cap and red-striped trousers, who started off by asking me (in French) if I would give him a bottle or two. I told him I would give him a thick ear or two, but the benighted man did not understand Glaswegian. About ten minutes later I wandered round behind some cases that were piled up, and found my French friend carefully secreting one under some sacking. That sort of thing went on all the blessed day till I was nearly attacking some of them.

It has been decided to change the engineer, so I conveyed the news to him. We have wired for two from home. Struck our top-masts today. Don't want them in winter in the Atlantic. Old man thinks it may ease our rolling a bit if we leave them here. About four in the afternoon the graft merchants decided that we might as well put back what we had taken out, about 5,600 cases. Worked on at that till 7:30 p.m., when most of the Frenchmen in one of the holds had to be assisted out, much to the annoyance of certain members of our crew who had not had their opportunities.

I have now got an assistant supercargo, an Australian, who is studying medicine in his spare time. He is making the trip and will act as doctor should the occasion arise. Don't think his medical knowledge is very profound; it can't be, as I think he is only in his second year; but he seems a decent chap.

The skipper had a field-day today. The cook had managed to get hold of some whisky, and got himself into a fine condition; then he thought it would be a useful thing to go on the bridge and give cheek to the Old Man. Well, he did so. Skipper stood it for some time. Then his patience wore out and he rushed at him, got him by the throat, dragged him behind the charthouse, and gave him just as fine a hiding as ever he got in his life; and if ever a man asked for it, he did. This was in view of most of the Frenchmen, who yelled and shouted with excitement. It's a wonder we hadn't to fish for some of them in the water. The cook was signed off later on.

About nine the doctor man and myself went off to have a look round Havre. We wandered into the Casino, but did not play, as we hadn't enough money. Got back to the ship at 3:15 a.m. I'm going to be tired in the morning.

9th September.—Sunday, but that doesn't matter. Started loading again at 7:30, and got finished about 11:30. I thought I should manage to have a quiet afternoon, and possibly get a wee sleep, but Fate and the boss were all against that idea, not to mention all the writing I had to do. There is a damned sight more clerical work to be done on this boat than I had bargained for. I shall be running a shop, I find (in sea parlance, the slop-chest)—tobacco, cigarettes, matches, shirts, writing-paper, socks, etc.—also the official log and all the crew accounts. I believe the proper appellation for my job is "ship's husband."

Well, about six I had got through with listening to a homily from the boss on how to clean ports and chip old paint.

He has presented aft with seven bottles of whisky, and so far he and his friends have managed to scoff off three of them. The other four are to see us across the Atlantic. What a hope! I can see us having none left before we start, if he comes about the ship any more.

Our late cook came down tonight to see if he could get a meal and a bed on board, as he has spent his passage money and is now on the beach. Havre, I should think, is a bad place in which to be on the beach. The skipper got him and hunted him for his life off the ship. He jerked him out of the galley like a whelk out of his shell, flung him on to the quay, then extended a cordial invitation to him to come on board again and have it out, which invitation I may say was not accepted.

About 7:30 the doctor and I wandered into Havre in search of food and distraction for a couple of hours. We landed in a small restaurant in one of the main boulevards, and, as they would not change British money and we had very little French, it was a case of adding up before ordering. We thought we were ordering a special kind of sole, but it turned out to be fresh-water mussels cooked in a kind of onion sauce. They were very good, however, and we managed the lot. Adjourned from there to a café where there is music. Sat and listened to that for a bit; then back to the boat.

10th September.—Nothing special until five, when it was decided we would go out to a buoy in the bay and lie there all night. The crew are much disappointed, as they had the idea they would get so many francs each and be able to have somewhat of a jamboree for the last night.

At seven our engines were performing their allotted task. There was no steam in the donkey, as the feed pump is being repaired, so we had to warp her out by hand, a deuce of a job, as we were well at the end of the docks and had numerous right-angle turnings to negotiate.

Our new chief engineer arrived today, and also the second— both good fellows. We signed on a Norwegian as cook, and two deckhands who are gentlemen from Finland, and look it.

Got out to our moorings just as dusk was falling. Somehow or another our worthy gentlemen who live in the fo'c'sle have managed to obtain refreshment and are showing signs of having a night of it. Had a yarn with the skipper, and arranged to share watch with the mate and Doc Second mate and bos'n are one, and, as he has had some rum with the crew, skipper decided not to have him on deck.

My watch was from one to four. The fun in the fo'c'sle was fast and furious when I took over. It appears that our Finnish friends had brought several bottles of rum on board.

At 3 a.m. Mr. Martin, an elderly gentleman, with a tarry, misspent life behind him, and the same in front, I should think, came out and sat on the forehatch and sang psalms for quite a long time. His rendering of Old Hundredth was particularly fine, with an accompaniment of hiccoughs coming in just at the proper moment.

> All (hic) people that on (hic) earth do dwell,
> Sing to the (hic), etc., etc.

About 3:30 a.m. a small steamer of an enquiring turn of mind came across to interview us, and shouted to know who we were and all about us. As I thought there might be some Customs difficulty, I refrained from giving them information beyond the fact that my reply was "Me no comprenez," which statement they could do what they liked with. They sheered off alter about five minutes of this, and went to seek sympathy from other shipping that were anchored near us.

Had a yarn with the mate, who came to relieve me at 4:15 a.m., also a cup of coffee, and turned in half an hour later.

CHAPTER IV

'RENDEZVOUS'

11th September.—A dense fog in the morning; could hardly see the bow from aft. Cleared about eleven, when the owner arrived in a tug. Got my final instructions. He brought two volumes of obscure French poetry, from which we have selected certain pages, the words of which will be used as code words on any orders that are sent from him on shore on the other side. I keep one copy and he the other. We shook hands, and then we started off on our three-thousand-mile journey to the rendezvous.

Crew not feeling at all well today. When repacking cases down in the forehold, several piteous appeals for alcohol had to be turned down. By ten tonight we should have been well within sight of Cherbourg Light, but, as it had coyly decided to remain hidden, we hove to and took soundings. Found 27 fathoms, which was too shallow, so proceeded very cautiously. About an hour later we saw a glimmer of the light about three points away from where it should have been. The current is very strong here, and, as we are a wee bit down by the head, owing to the re-stowage of our cargo, we had been carried out of our course a little.

Nothing to report except the common incidents of travel. Sighted a big German liner, three funnels, and, as we passed quite close to it, I managed to get two photos. Spent most of the day making up my store-books and men's accounts which I have to keep, also studying the B.O.T. scale of rations, as I am officer commanding stores. Have not had any time yet to read anything. Had a sleep for two hours in the afternoon, which I badly needed. A glorious day; not a cloud and very warm. Will turn in early tonight.

12th September.—A most amusing incident today. Went on to the bridge about 7 a.m. Second mate on watch. It was a fine morning, so we "greeted" each other. If it hadn't been fine we would just have grunted.

"Come here a minute, mister," said Mr. Jones, retiring to the end of the bridge remote from the charthouse door. "What's the matter with the old man this morning?"

"I don't know. How do you mean?"

"Well, since six he has been swearing like a trooper, and has had every chart on the ship out half a dozen times, I'm sure. Now, you know there is something like fifty charts in there, so what's he looking for? Jings! Just listen to that. What do you think of it? Fine, man, eh?"

It was! I hadn't realized until now what charts could really do in their spare time.

Eight bells. Breakfast.

After breakfast I went back to the bridge, peeped into the charthouse through a port, and could just make out the Old Man surrounded by 'blue backs' and Admiralty charts by the score. About an hour later bang opens the charthouse door and out he comes in a perfect hurricane of purple language, stamps to the other end of the bridge, says it all over again, then back to me.

"Look here, Mister Man, I've just opened my secret instructions, and the 'carmen-tinted' idiot who wrote them has given me a place to go to that isn't marked on any 'unmentionable' chart on this giddy ship. I've been all over the world and never heard of the place before. It's some ruddy Spanish word, I think. Come in and look at it for yourself."

He led the way, and, stepping over the pile of 'blue backs' on the floor, picked up a letter, and read to me as follows:

"'Dear Captain,—When you reach the Rendezvous you will, etc.'

"Now, mister, where in hell is Rendezvous, for I can't find it?"

Poor old chap. It was a terrible job to keep a straight face and explain that it was only a name that the rum-runners had given to the part of the American coast off Long Island. But it was most infernally funny. From a later passage in the letter it appears we are to make for a point due S.E. Ambrose Light and eight miles from it.

CHAPTER V

A STIFF BLOW

14th September.—This old packet can roll to some tune. Was nearly decanted from my bunk several times during the night. We are not off the banks yet; they run out for about four hundred miles west of the entrance to the Channel. The consequence is that you get a very nasty sea sometimes, and we certainly had one today. About eleven I advised the Doc to go and see that nothing was adrift in our room (he sleeps on the settee in the saloon). He was just in time to see tumblers, a water-jug and a flower-pot—containing a fern that died, I think, in the early 'seventies—all take a beautiful header on to the floor, where they met an untimely end.

The wind died away at noon, so we took down all sails, as the Old Man can't stand the noise the gaffs make banging from side to side with every roll. I felt like a broken-winded cab-horse, for it is about as difficult to take them down as to put them up, since we have to put the down-hauls over the barrel of a winch and wind them down. About two the wind took on again W.N.W., so we put the damned things all up again. It takes two and a quarter hours to put the boom sails up, using the hand-gear on the winches. It is a great game played slow, when there is no steam. We must conserve our coal for unloading at the other side. Got them up at 4:30—two and a half hours to put up three large sails. However, she is a fine sea boat. We ship very little water; only once was I up to the waist, and that was in backlash off the hatch coamings.

We have made about 350 miles since leaving Havre, which is not so bad. Had a small concert tonight. Played away at my chanter for a bit, and had another shot at the concertina. Got on a bit better with it. The clatter of the wash-ports is like a shipyard with a thousand riveters at work.

15th September.—Saturday, but no going out to Hampden to see the Queen's. Blowing fairly stiffly from the N.W. Messed about with the sails—a short sentence, but it meant about two hours' fairly hard work. That is really all I have to say about today. McLeod is ill, so there's one man off a three-man watch and more deck work for me. Hope he gets better soon. 10 p.m. Wind is rising a bit, and it looks rather like a dirty night.

16th September.—Sunday, not much rest about today. I was correct about the dirty night, in fact about 3 a.m. one of our sails, the mizzen-boom sail, was blown nearly to ribbons; the main-boom sail also split, but it is at least repairable. The second mate, who is a sail-maker, has been turned on to stitch up the mainsail, and has a full day's job and more before him. He is sitting up on No. 2 hatch working at it, as there's too much water messing about on the deck.

We have an interesting crowd aboard. They have all seen most of the world, and like pulling my leg about experiences here, there and everywhere. I have heard something about every quarter of the world, barring perhaps the Arctic and Antarctic regions.

The wind is shifting. About midday the N. wind died down and a puff or two was coming from the W. At nine we were hardly making any headway; all canvas down and engines going full ahead. Had a chat with the skipper on our prospects. With two sails blown out, the other big one starting to split, and no spares that are worth anything on board, it doesn't look very rosy. The Azores are the nearest land on our route, but they are about eight hundred miles off. If this W. wind gets harder they might as well be eight thousand for all the good they will do.

I took watch on the bridge from eight bells till midnight. When I left Mr. Mate took over, and at that time we could barely maintain her head to the wind. Had a cup of cocoa and turned in at 12:45 a.m. I had suggested to the skipper that the only alternative to making the Azores was to turn about and try to make a Channel port and get new canvas; but the idea did not commend itself—in fact, he said he had never turned back yet, and wasn't going to now, though he admits that if this wind freshens to a gale we shall be helpless before it, and make mighty valuable salvage for someone. I thought so too.

CHAPTER VI

DIRTY WEATHER

17th September.—Was wakened at 6 a.m. by the skipper and went on deck to find a westerly gale in full blast and the *Cask* running before it. Glass dropping rapidly. The situation has assumed a more serious aspect. We can't heave her to and ride it out, for she won't stay put, but just lies broadside to the sea. As a matter of fact, the sea is too big now to try and 'bout ship. The engines can't keep her head up, so we are driving straight for the Bay of Biscay somewhere. Unless the wind changes considerably we shall be in a mess in forty-eight hours. At ten the wind backed a bit to W.S.W., but is still far too strong to risk our last pieces of canvas; however, it lets us get the bowsprit pointing nearer to the entrance to the Channel.

Had a long talk with the captain, who takes rather a serious view of the situation. The Azores are now out of the question, and I suggested we should make Falmouth if we can. After some talk he agreed that this was the only thing to do, so we are *en route*. There is a very dirty sea running now; one big fellow came over the poop, and I thought it would smash in the companion door to the cabin aft, but it didn't. All day we raced along with bare poles at 9-1/4 knots. A full gale, as seamen call it, is now blowing. Personally, I shall be quite content not to see any that are fuller. It doesn't look like getting to the Channel unless this wind backs a bit more.

I'm feeling a bit seedy; hope it isn't seasickness.

The Old Man hasn't been exactly good company for the last two days; in fact, he has been rubbing down our throats that we are for the beach somewhere north of Biarritz. Not quite sure if he's trying a leg-pull; if he is, he's acting the part dam' well.

18th September.—Took a dose of bromide last night to try to make myself sleep. It is up to me to a certain extent to say whether we should go on at this season of the year, and I'm damned if I can make my mind up whether to risk it or not. About 5:20 a.m. the wind suddenly moderated and, glory be, backed to S.S.W., so we had an early start and got two jibs and the trysail up. It was all we dared put up at the moment. One of the torn sails has been patched sufficiently to last, perhaps, an hour, long enough in a pinch to get us round a knuckle. The glass is very slowly rising, and we have hopes of being able to make our port without much further trouble. At three the wind had eased sufficiently to enable the fore-boom sail to be set, and we are now on a course to take us into the Channel, steering N.E.1/2N. Tomorrow evening, if all goes well, should see us off the Lizard Light. The boss sails tomorrow on the *Olympic*, so we should pass him somewhere off the Channel. I can imagine what he will feel like when he sights us coming back. It is his own fault for sending a ship to sea with no decent spare canvas.

Our decks for the last three days have been like miniature Niagaras, and one has to watch out and not meet a mass of water arriving over the coamings. The air compressor in the engineroom is showing signs of giving out.

19th September.—The days are coming in and going out, and I see them doing it most of the time. We don't get much sleep at present. Got up at 5:30, and started in to get a very hastily patched sail up just half-way in case it would go like the rest. Won't be in today after all. The wind has dropped very considerably and a little less swell is running. I thought we were over once this afternoon, all the same. We took a roll that sent the starboard coamings well under, and another on the top of it that nearly did the trick. I fixed a gimlet eye on a likely spar, but she came up after thinking the matter over. We are making a lot of leeway. Today has amounted to about thirty-eight miles (too much).

CHAPTER VII

BACK TO PORT

20th September.—This has been rather a humorous day. Firstly we couldn't make Falmouth, and had to come on to the next port on the map, which I think is a better place, in any case. I went and shaved, and got myself looking pretty to go ashore and wire sundry people that the Swift Saloon Vessel *Cask* had arrived here. I have practically no money, so I'll need to look for a nice kind pawnbroker with a philanthropic turn of mind and lend him my watch. The pilot took us in, and we anchored about seven. Our next guests to arrive were the Customs, and I had to make myself agreeable and get our tobacco, etc., passed. During the Customs visitation they spotted a case under the Australian mutton and asked, "What's that?" I didn't want to tell them (as I thought it was the 'great secret'—a machine-gun). How ever, they insisted, so out it had to come. Luckily it merely contained a smoke helmet with respirator and its fixings. I am sure they thought I was trying to be funny. I wonder where in hell the machine-gun is? I hadn't intended having it out until we were clear of soundings. Got that done about 8:30 p.m., and went ashore with them. Bade them an affectionate farewell at the pier and went off to send my wires. After that I found I had 2s. 6d. left to get food and lodging. I'm going to have one night ashore. Tried several hotels, but, as I had no luggage, they all wanted a deposit, and didn't seem to look on me with favour when I offered my watch as security. After the eighth attempt I found a benevolent lady who presides over the happiness of her guests at Marshall's Hotel. As she asked no deposit I got in there, and was very comfortable. Went out and had a look round the town in the dark. Got back to the hotel at 10:30 p.m., had a wee one, and went to bed.

21st September.—Sneaked out first thing after breakfast, when no one was looking, to find my benevolent pawnbroker. Unearthed a gentleman with the fine old Highland name of Isaac and trafficked with him for shekels of silver in exchange for my watch. That gave me £3. Got off my wireless to the boss on the *Olympic* and other messages. Hired a motorboat and went off to the ship; found a perfectly splendid hullabaloo going on. The Customs people, coming out to seal up our tea and lime-juice, had found a cake of tobacco in among some matches, and were threatening to put all kinds of innocent people in court and take their hard-earned money from them. However, with the aid of diplomacy and the magical sum of £2 I squared them off. I am told that the official who discovers dutiable goods after everything has been sealed up gets that sum. I think I am having my leg pulled, but it's better than a row. They are coming back at 3 p.m. to collect their ill-gotten gains. This means another visit to Mr. Isaac. Saw them off, and went away in my motorboat a little later. Told my boatman to be ready for me at 2:15, and went off to see Mr. Isaac. Got £3 on my cigarette case, had lunch on the strength of it, and got a dozen loaves of bread for the ship. Customs arrived about 3:30. Got them squared up and went ashore to look out for telegrams. Motor boats are expensive things here: 10*s.* a time. By this time I had nearly exhausted my other £3, so had another interview with my friend from Jerusalem and got £3 5*s.* on my chain. I was now in funds and could pay my hotel bill if necessary, and also go and have a dashed good dinner.

Well, I had that at a place called the 'Globe,' where I watched a lot of dizzy dancing. Got back to hotel about ten. A gentleman from Glasgow is arriving tomorrow. My friend Mr. Cork, to whom I wired for money, has not yet put in an appearance; at least, the cash hasn't. My Glasgow friend, who is a shipping agent, when I reported my cash difficulties, told me I was a damned fool. Why did I not go to a proper shipping agent, who would have looked after me at once? Well, we're always learning. A proper agent is now appointed.

There is more in this than meets the eye. I had not realized that this would be an underwriter's job, but so it seems. My Glasgow gentleman had arrived with a Mr. Main, a surveyor. Spent the evening with them going over the whole business.

23rd September.—It's a game, it's a game. Spent part of the forenoon at the boat going over things. The procedure appears to be that Main makes the damage as much as possible, while the underwriter's surveyor makes it as little as he can; then the average adjusters come in and assess according to what they think of each surveyor's report, while I stand and look on at the battle. I can see this diary isn't going to last out if I write so much each day, so it will require to be curtailed. Drank a certain amount of whisky and spent a lot of pennies in automatic machines on the pier, which neither worked nor gave us our pennies back.

24th September.—Busy today. A Captain Sealy, who has been appointed by Lloyds' Surveyors, managed to get skipper on Friday to let him have a look at the scrap log before our man had seen it, which he had no damned business to do. This was rather unfortunate, but we'll see. Spent day on sail plan and specification of new sails for which we have wired off to London. Expect they will be down on Thursday morning. Good thing I'm living ashore, as, with the damage and the new sails and ropes arriving, I would only be in the way on board. Anyhow, there's plenty to do ashore.

25th September.—Nothing humorous. Our agent went off back to Glasgow, and Main and I are carrying on. Went to a show at the Palace in the evening. Quite good.

26th September.—Row with Board of Trade. Some member of the crew who is evidently a sea lawyer has reported that the ship's boats are insufficient. It appears that in a vessel of this size, that only carries two boats, each must be capable of taking the whole crew. Well, we are seventeen, and one boat only takes fourteen and the other twelve. So we have to put a 'class C' on board, where it will make a dashed nuisance of itself perched on No.1 hatch.

27th September.—Same old grind. Spent part of the day looking for a new galley range. The cooking has been appalling, and the fault is partly the range, which is failing to pieces. Saw *The Lady of the Rose* in the evening.

28th September.—Sails and ropes have arrived and have gone on board.

29th September.—Expected to sail today. Met the wee gentleman from Glasgow at 10 a.m., and we proceeded on board after I had signed up all my accounts. There we found they couldn't get the donkey-pump to suck and that there was no steam to lift the anchor. Also the silencer on the engine has developed a crack that must be repaired, so the engineers have an all-night job ahead of them. The agent, Main and self decided to go and see how they were getting on about 8:30 p.m. With some difficulty we got a motorboat, which promptly caught fire as we were starting, so we had to look for another one. Finally got aboard at 11:20 p.m., and back to the hotel about midnight.

CHAPTER VIII

RUNNING SOUTH

30th September.–At last we are off. It has been a busy week, but as I write this we are about sixty-five miles on our three-thousand-mile run. Our old mate had to go home ill, and we have shipped another, who should be a good man if ugliness counts for anything. Had to pay off our hymn-singing hand, ill—McLeod too, a dashed good fellow—more's the pity. To replace them we wired to Havre for two more Finns, so that the fo'c'sle now contains three Finns, one Swede (Kelly), and two Glasgow lads who are good fellows, plus the two stowaways.

Sailing peacefully along through a fairly dense mist which is rather damp. I found in port when weighing myself that I have managed to get my weight down by 16-1/2 lbs. since leaving Glasgow. That speaks well for getting fit, anyhow. We are heading S.W. 1/2W., which will take us clear of Ushant by about forty miles. Hope the Bay receives us kindly. Found two more stowaways this morning. Captain does not quite know what to do with them, so we will keep them for the present; they are both very seasick and very sorry for themselves.

1st October.—The miles march on. Tonight we are 324 miles out and are bowling along at just over seven knots, which is good as the wind is not strong. Spent a good part of the day with the mate, putting the lifeboats in proper order. Found the great secret, i.e., a machine-gun, under the bottom of the bath, and had it to pieces. It is in good working order, but, as it is a German one, our .303 won't fit it; also there are no cartridge belts for it, so it isn't going to be of much service. There is very little swell tonight.

2nd October.—The gentleman in charge of Mr. Bolinder (our pro-
pelling agent) came to me today and said he hadn't enough lubricat-
ing oil for the crossing. Why the dickens he couldn't have asked for
this before we left port beats me. We are using eleven gallons in twenty-four hours, and will now have to put into Madeira, where I expect
the inhabitants will charge us no mean price. Captain has decided, in
any case, to take the southerly course and try to find those kindly people known as the N.E. Trades. The *Cask* could never manage the great
circle course from the Channel at the equinoctial season. Well, in any
case, we've tried and we've had some.

3rd October.—A good day, N.N.W. wind moderate. Yesterday
and until midday today we have logged 190 miles, which is very
good going. We are now just south of Cape Finisterre, which is the
southern arm of the Bay of Biscay, so that is a bad bit over. Passed
through numerous shoals of fish after dark; they were just like a
luminous mist under the water, and could be seen as far off as 200
yards. Have made a small chart to show our wanderings.

We are making for Madeira; in any case, our course was only
thirty miles W. of it, so we are putting in there for some more lubri-
cating oil and to land the latest two stowaways; also I shall be able
to get some letters off. Our exact position at midday today was
40.56 N. x 12.15 W. Now we all know exactly where we are.

4th October.—A glorious day, very hot. We are getting along fine.
At noon were well south of latitude 40°, which puts us nearly due
west of the Straits of Gibraltar. Spent most of today sorting out potatoes on the forehatch. An exciting job!

A perfect night. Our old friend the Plough is very low in the
north. Saw a very beautiful sight tonight. The sea was practically
calm, only light southerly airs; we were under power and moving
about four knots. About four bells in the evening watch came a cry
from the bridge, "Sail ahead!" Hard over to starboard. The 'sail' was
a three-masted square rigger, all sail set and no lights. She was like
a ghost as she went past, the phosphorescence from the slight ripple throwing a rather ghostly light on her sails, which was reflected
in the water. The only light visible on board was thrown by the binnacle, which shone on the face of the steersman as he drowsed (or

appeared to) over the wheel. "What price the ruddy *Flying Dutchman*, Mac?" shouted the mate from the bridge. And, by gum! she might have been.

5th October.—Saturday, I was appealed to by the mate and captain this morning as to what day it was. So, as it was Saturday (I know that from my barometric readings, for every four hours I jot down on a chart my reading of the barometer), I told them the truth, with the result that all but necessary labour on board ceased at 12 noon. Had my bagpipes out, and did about half an hour's work at them. Had all my blankets and mattress out also and gave them a thorough sunning. Glorious day. Still very warm; wind N. by E., but pretty light. Should sight Madeira tomorrow afternoon.

The Old Man has fairly got a down on the engineroom staff. I was on the bridge this evening when the engine suddenly coughed spasmodically once or twice and then stopped.

"Look here, mister," said the captain, "what the hell do these bums do down there all day? If that oily-fingered chief comes up here with any of his damned silly stories, I'll tell him who his mother was, who he is, and where he'll go when he is dead."

Fortunately he had hardly announced his intentions when there was a prodigious bang from aft, and a beautiful smoke-ring shot up from the jigger mast as the engine started off again.

"I think, captain," I said, "it must just have been an air lock in the fuel piping; it is nothing to worry about, and a thing that can easily happen."

"Ach, hell with them!" was all the answer I got, as he stamped off to the other end of the bridge.

CHAPTER IX

AT MADEIRA

6th October.—Sighted Madeira at 2:30 p.m., about forty miles off. Engine got tired about 4 p.m. and sat down for a rest. We allowed it to rest for an hour or two, as it was no use trying to get in after dark, having no charts of the place. Abreast of the island at eight, and spent the night dodging about.

7th October.—A glorious morning. Motored round the E. end of the island and made for Funchal. Extraordinary place Madeira. A large, deeply creviced volcanic rock with a thin layer of soil, which the natives make the most of. Houses everywhere, most of them in positions where you would think they would roll over into the water. Very precipitous. It is about thirty miles long by about fifteen broad.

Motored into Funchal at 6:30 a.m. and dropped anchor. Perspiring Portuguese immediately swarmed round us trying to sell us basket chairs with one hand and steal our ropes with the other. A gentleman called da Murta arrived on board and announced he was the most honest man in the world and did all the business in the place and would be honoured to swindle us if I made him our agent. I did so, as he was willing to send cables without my giving him the money for them. Went ashore with him and got my cables off.

This is a most interesting place. Narrow streets paved with round stones off the beach, each one projecting about one inch up and polished, purposely I expect, for the benefit of the unwary stranger. A most appalling set of cut-throats the whole gang of them. Our boatman hasn't shaved for about a fortnight and looks as though murder was a fine art with him.

Went and interviewed the British Consul about our two stowaways.

They have promptly disappeared down the forepeak. The Consul doesn't appreciate 'Wandering Willies' of that sort, and I don't blame him. He says we shall have to pay their passage home. We will dump them and see what happens. Wandered about a bit, had a smell at the fish market, and looked at the fruit market. A popular method of conveyance is a bullock arrangement on skids like a sledge, with a very elaborate body like a gondola at the Edinburgh carnival. The bullocks are very small, and all have the tips of their horns pierced for reins.

Ordered fresh meat, etc., and went on board. Men want to go ashore, but nothing doing. Kelly is making trouble, and I think will require attending to. This place looks very pretty at night with all the lights lit, making patterns on the hillsides, which are about two thousand feet high and as steep as the deuce. Had a chat with the skipper, who has the wind up a bit about the crew. Then I turned in.

8th October.—Damn! fleas have arrived. I think about 324 have got into my bunk; at least, I spent a good part of the night scratching and am all bites this morning.

Went ashore to see if there was any reply to my cables, and got one. This is a den of thieves. I can't get oil under £12 10s. a barrel, so I must just pay that. I was sure we were going to have some trouble with the crew. Our Finnish hands managed to sell some kegs of paint and ropes over the side during last night, and went ashore in defiance of the captain's instructions this morning. Later the Doc and I went ashore to do some business and have a look around. Near the Consulate we ran into most of the crew, some of them merry on the rum they got in exchange for our paint. We were immediately surrounded, and demands for money were made. I refused, on the Old Man's instructions, and Kelly immediately threatened violence, promised me he and I would be enemies and I could use my weapons and he would use his. I will. Got rid of them after a good deal of trouble, in which broaching cargo was a detail.

Our Portuguese friend is rather amusing. When in his office today the skipper of a collier came in. The most honest man in the world is acting as her agent also. Mr. da Murta suggested an adjournment to his private bonded store, where he assured us we would taste such Madeira that the 'houris' would envy, even though they are supposed to be teetotal. Not being able to speak Portuguese, I merely said "Lead on, MacDuff." He led on; and certainly the Madeira he produced from a large hogshead was wonderful. So wonderful that when I got outside Funchal appeared to be revolving in an orbit of its own, of which I was one of the foci. Got back to the office with difficulty. My friend the captain of the collier departed, after arranging to meet me later. Then the reason for the old Madeira was made apparent by Senhor da Murta, who suggested to me that I should swap 1,000 cases of Mr. John Dewar for 1,000 cases of his wonderful Madeira. He only made one mistake, and that was in appraising my affection for Mr. Dewar. So he was informed that the answer was in the negative. We both lifted our hats to each other—at least, I lifted a Harris tweed cap and he flourished a damp Panama.

Later I met my collier friend. We had one, and I asked him if he could do with two cabin boys. Gave him their history as far as I knew it. He said he could. "Look here, old man, you bring them ashore tonight at eight, and I'll have a boat waiting with three men who will attend to them." "Righto!" says I. At eight the two were handed over as per programme. I'm quite sure they will think that the sea is an overrated pastime.

Went back on board. About 10 p.m. a very scared member of the crew arrived and told us most of the others had been chased and stoned, and that three were in jail. I am not surprised. Made arrangements to deal with Kelly tomorrow.

9th October.—Watched the fo'c'sle most of the night to see that no more oil or paint was sold overboard. Turned in to my friends the fleas about 4:30 a.m. All our oil is aboard, and it only remains to get the money to pay for it.

Went ashore early and fixed up with the Consul. Paid Kelly off, and then squared my account with the Portuguese philanthropist with whom we have been dealing.

Have signed on a curious bird. A tall, lean lad came up to me today and asked if there was any chance of a job on board our yacht. Well, as we had just got rid of one deckhand I told him I would ask the skipper. He has told me he has been to sea and can steer a course, and that he is also a trained engineer. His nationality is

Dutch. I fancy he has left happy Dutchland for the benefit of Dutchland. He appears desperately anxious to get to America. Spoke to the skipper an signed him on.

Got ten bottles of wine out of Mr. da Murta as a present to divide between the captain and self. Madeira wine, not bad, but just a little heady and heavy.

Today this place is absolutely stifling, not a breath of air, and some of the odours are the limit. Got squared up and out to the ship at one o'clock.

IN THE N.E. TRADES

LOOKING FOR BERMUDAS

CHAPTER X

THE CROSSING

10th October.—Heaved up the anchor and got off to sea at 2:30. All on board had a wee tot to celebrate our departure. Very little wind while in shelter of the island, but about four miles out it freshened up nicely and back into the N.E.

I am sleeping very badly just now, for some reason I can't fathom, for I go to bed tired enough. This little trip into Funchal has cost exactly £126 18*s*. 10*d*.—a bit thick when it could easily have been avoided. Turned in at 11:30.

11th October.—Fine breeze all night. Engine had to be stopped at six this morning, No. 1 cylinder blowing badly at the head. Engines off all day. Beautiful weather. Did a successful afternoon's washing of shirts, socks and towels. Stretched a line from the flagstaff to a davit and dried them. Only making about 2 knots, as the breeze is very light. Engine started up at 4:30, so now we are pegging along at the old pace again. Opened up our first barrel of salt beef; it looks very good, and will be tried tomorrow. Got some good fruit from Funchal. We actually had a new dish for breakfast—ham and eggs with fried bananas—and it was very good indeed. Must have it again before the bananas are done.

Fair job of work to do tomorrow. Overhaul the windlass on the fo'c'sle head. I served part of my apprenticeship in a windlass builder's shop. It should be a three days' job, I think. Peabody has managed to get a dog on board, so we have two mascots, the other being a kitten. It looks like a dachshund without the dash. Spends the day sleeping in a coil of rope.

12th October.—Rose like a belated lark about seven, and got busy at sorting the windlass, which is in a terrible condition. Half of it is out of action owing to rust, and the other half works when it suits itself. I said yesterday it would be a three days' job, but I fancy we shall be lucky if it is finished in five days—that is Tuesday or Wednesday, as Sunday on board is a *dies non* as far as work is concerned. We just sail the bally boat. Ran a big end in the engineroom, so engine is off for repairs. No wind, so we are not exactly rushing about the ocean. Worked at the windlass all day, and then had a spell in the engineroom till about midnight. Quite comfortably tired when I pushed off to bed.

13th October.—Another windlass day, also windless. Very hot. Knocked off work at noon and have just loafed round since then. Read up some navigation in the afternoon and had a wee sleep. Had a bath standing on the top of a life belt in my cabin! Can't use the bath, as she rolls all the water out at once. I think two or three more families of fleas have arrived in my bed. I am now bitten from head to foot, damn them! The wind is dead ahead, and we are well off our course again, heading for somewhere in the region of Brazil, I should say. Spent part of the night tidying up the saloon. The Old Man is getting the wind up already about West Indian hurricanes, and is studying the North Atlantic directory. Strikes me he is a bit previous, as we have about 2,300 miles yet before we reach the path of them. I believe they are rather unpleasant gentlemen, all the same. They will just require to be dealt with when the time comes.

Wind freshening a bit. Ran engine for half an hour, but bearing started heating badly, so shut down. Being Sunday, I taught myself to play 'Lead, Kindly Light' on the concertina. Getting on well with it. Glass falling; looks like a blow coming.

8 p.m., half a gale blowing, ship rolling very badly.

14th October.—Glass falling steadily. Gale now, with heavy seas. What a day! Every blessed thing on the ship has gone wrong. Firstly, at 7 a.m. discovered the engineroom half full of water. No engineer on watch at night, as they had been at it hard all day yesterday with two big ends. A leak somewhere. Started a bucket gang to bale it out. The Old Man is dancing mad, and like most square rig men, he thinks the engineroom staff is a coalition designed for his discomfiture. The deck-pump refused duty next. As the donkey-boiler has no water in it, we filled it with sea water in buckets by unscrewing the safety-valve. A long job. Blowing hard at midday, and looking not at all well. Making a tremendous lot of leeway. Got steam on the donkey bilge pump. Before that, started up the main engine so as to use her bilge pumps. After two hours' running she heated up; a main bearing this time. Not sure yet if it has run or not.

About three the wind suddenly ceased altogether, and we have been wallowing about in the trough of a big swell ever since. Dashed uncomfortable! Then the galley fire insisted on blowing out of the galley instead of up the chimney, and in consequence there was no hot dinner. Glass rising a little, but I don't think we have finished with the wind yet. Got engineroom clear of water about 9:30 p.m. Found one of the bilge valves not bedding in properly.

17th October.—For the last three days we have been rushing about the ocean in a perfectly scandalous way. The day before yesterday we made about eight miles on our course; yesterday we managed about three, and today about the same, days being periods of twenty-four hours. Worked all day at the windlass, and have nearly got the blessed thing in order. All the clutches are now free, and it just remains to pack the glands on the cylinders. Nothing of special interest. Glass is rising very slowly. Think I have got rid of the family of fleas that had taken up their abode in my bunk. At least, I have caught eight of them, and got no fresh bites last night. Learned to play 'The Minstrel Boy' and 'Ye Banks and Braes' tonight on the concertina. For about one and a half hours this afternoon there was a tremendous swell arriving down from the N.

Drifting about and doing nothing was the order of today. Engine won't be ready for a couple of days yet. Skipper sent our lean Dutchman down to the engineroom to lend a hand. He had stated in Madeira that he was an engineer, but he came up the engineroom ladder a great deal quicker than he went down, and, what's more, a two-inch spanner followed him. So evidently he is not an engineer. Spent most of the day at the windlass again. Broached cargo this morning to the extent of one case of Mr. Dewar. It is quite impossible to expect contentment forward, with all this stuff on board, if the crew are not to have a drink occasionally

18th October.—Nothing special doing. At the windlass again; nearly finished now. Dried codfish for dinner; most seem to like it, but I do not; it is abominable stuff, to my taste. The cook was in trouble today with his friends in the fo'c'sle, and I'm not surprised, for he's a rotten cook. They gave him a hammering, anyhow. He is a Norwegian, and one of the A.B.'s is a Swede.

The wind has died away, so we are just standing still. Sat on the after-wheel grating for a bit this evening and watched a lot of summer lightning, also a beautiful lunar rainbow. Have now learned to play most of 'The Rosary' on the concertina. Very heavy tropical showers tonight, and decks inclined to leak after the hot weather. We are at present about 150 miles due S. of the Azores.

19th October.–A quiet, peaceable day. Finished my job on the windlass. I hope the damned thing will work when the steam is turned on. I shall require to test it before we need to drop our anchor. Did some odd jobs about the ship and engine-room. Practised the concertina in the evening.

20th October.—Had the best sleep last night I have had for a long time. Got up about 7:15 a.m. Nothing much doing in the forenoon. Made a barometer card to fix over the one in the cabin, as it is not graded in inches but in some foreign way I don't understand, so it doesn't tell me much. That took most of the forenoon. Read a book most of the afternoon. Received an inspiration for a design for an illuminated letterhead, and started on to that. Engine got underway about five. Two of the bearings a little hot, but they will cool down all right, I think. A glorious night. Second mate saw a sleeping turtle floating past this forenoon. That constituted Saturday.

21st October.—Sunday, have spent practically all day at my illumination. The only time I was off it was when the Old Man decided to take down all sails and, three hours later, put them all up again. There has been a decent breeze all day—just enough to prevent it becoming too hot. A lot of Gulf weed floating past. This week has gone on at a deuce of a pace; it seems no time since last Sunday. Can now play the trio of Chopin's Funeral March—a nice cheery thing to sit and play on a moonlight night. Lot of meteors about, also the stormy petrels have returned and are following the ship. Bad cess to them!

Did some odd jobs this afternoon, such as polishing the after binnacle. Engine started up again and going great guns; must be doing close on 7 knots. Have an idea this won't last very long. Very hot again.

22nd October.—Quite an interesting day. Was up on the fo'c'sle head looking over when I spotted what is called a pilot fish—a funny-looking chap, marked with brown and grey stripes, as though he was wearing a football jersey. It was swimming along just in front of the stem, and keeping about a foot off it. These fish, I believe, always keep company with a shark, and act as pilot and scout. When there is danger, they bolt into the shark's mouth. Mr. Shark is probably in the vicinity of the boat, although we haven't seen him. I got three hooks (large ones) and made up a line, baited with a big lump of pork fat. When the engines stop again, I may have a chance to get the shark alongside, if I am lucky enough to hook him. The only thing I have caught so far is a bunch of Gulf weed, which may go into a bottle as a souvenir.

Perfect night; full moon. Old Man in a very bad humour. The sails flap-flapping don't help to make him any better. Hope they manage to fix this blessed engine tomorrow, as I'm getting tired of this bit of ocean.

23rd October.—Wet morning, but cleared about ten. Got engines going at eleven, and they have managed to keep going. Saw an extraordinary thing tonight about 7 p.m. Was sitting on the after-wheel grating when a pear-shaped ball of fire, or something of that sort, materialised about amidships, floated past us about 50 yds. off and, say, 30 ft. from the water. It kept glowing and darkening, and left a faint trail like a meteor behind it. Did this three times before fading away; during this period it had perhaps moved 60 yds. Four of us saw it, but no one on the ship knows what it was. Nothing else of interest. Lost forty miles in the last twenty-four hours.

Even the prosaic business of sailing a 'fore and after' across the wintry ocean is relieved by some things that are funny. Our Long

Dutchman is in the port watch, and until today had not done a trick at the wheel. At eight bells, the first dog watch, he was told to go and relieve at the wheel. Half an hour later, when the Old Man came on the bridge, the man at the wheel complained to him that he had not yet been relieved. Skipper went on the hunt to see who should have relieved him, and found it was the ruddy Dutchman. There is an emergency wheel on the poop, which, of course, is not kept in gear. Mr. Dutchman was found solemnly gazing into the after binnacle, sawing the spokes of this wheel, and firmly imagining he was steering the ship. His departure from the poop was both involuntary and hurried, and I know he missed every rung of the ladder down to the well-deck. So we also know now that he is not a sailor as well as not an engineer.

24th October.—Fine day; very little wind. Skipper told me there was a shark round the ship the other day, as he had seen its fin. However, it ignored my lump of fat, so we'll ignore him. Started a new idea today, *i.e.*, making a tablecloth out of a piece of canvas. I am going to try to ornament it after the style of 'The Book of Kells.' It will be a long job, as the canvas is heavy and my thread and needle are represented by tarred twine and a sailmaker's needle. Worked at that for most of the evening.

26th October.—Friday again, and tomorrow Saturday. I wouldn't mind a round of golf, but will need to wait for a bit. All sails were taken in during the night, so, in accordance with the round game the skipper plays at, they were all put up again shortly after breakfast. Putting up the mainsail takes 1,047 turns of No. 2 winch, using hand-gear: I counted them today.

A fine day; wind has shifted into the N.E., the first fair wind we have had since leaving Funchal. Had a lesson in knots and splices from the second mate, who is also bos'n. Continued and finished the first portion of my tablecloth, *i.e.*, an ornamental circle with a representation of the *Cask* in the centre. Took mainsail down at 8:30, flapping rather badly, also the inner jib and fore topmast staysail. Putting them up again will be the first job to do in the morning, I expect.

27th October.—At 7:15 this morning along comes Mercury, disguised as P. Peters, A.B., with the captain's compliments, and will I assist to hoist the mainsail? That, of course, being just what we expected, no one was disappointed. After that there was nothing much doing. I sat in a lifeboat for about two hours and watched dozens of flying-fish knocking about—peculiar creatures of an average size of seven to eight inches. With the sun shining on them, they look like silver torpedoes skimming about two to five feet above the waves. Can't make out their wings, as they move too fast. Apparently they fall back into the water directly after their wings dry.

Fair wind most of the day, so engines were stopped for a bit to give the poor things a rest. The Old Man has been in a most genial mood, for some reason or other. It is the first time I have seen him smile for days. "Mister," he said to me, "what about a game of draughts?"

Now, captain is an expert, I believe; anyhow, he has several volumes lying about showing how the game should be played. It flashed through my mind that the engineer, who was on board while the ship was in Glasgow, had told me that a mate who was standing by had had a board broken over his head on one occasion, and, what was more, no longer 'stood by' Still, I didn't think that would happen, so I said, "All right, captain." We adjourned to the saloon, where I got out the men and a board (cardboard), and we started.

I moved. He replied. Then my turn again. "Oh!" he said, "that's the Auld Fourteenth you're playing." I didn't know what the mischief he was talking about, but said nothing, just playing again when it was my turn. "What the hell's that move?" he asked, glaring at me. "*That's* not the Auld Fourteenth; that move's not in the book." By pure chance I won the game.

He rose, and, taking a book from a drawer, slammed it down on the table, saying, "Look here, mister, you read that." Then he stamped away back to the charthouse. The book was a treatise on how to play draughts, and every possible game seemed to be fully described. On page 16 I found the solution to the Old Man's remarks: 'Game No. 14. This game is often called the Old Fourteenth.' So that was what he meant. My unorthodox move had completely upset the poor 'Auld Fourteenth,' which the Old Man, I think, must have looked on as verging on sacrilege.

At midday we were 1,145 miles from Bermudas. That, at least, is the distance if we manage to keep a proper course, which, to put it mildly, is highly improbable. Gave the crew a good nip at six, after which they held a sing-song forward during the whole of the second dog watch. Wind is inclined to get ahead a bit; shifted from S.E. to about S. by W. Hope it doesn't get any more to the W., or the 1,145 miles will quickly become twelve or thirteen hundred.

28th October.—Made 158 miles and 20 miles of leeway in the last twenty-four hours. Sunday is always washing-day, so we all turned washer women for the forenoon. The ship is decorated with shirts, handkerchiefs, three pairs of pajamas, socks, etc., etc. Fine drying wind. Still plenty of flying-fish about. At eight a squall struck us, accompanied by torrential rain. Wind shifted to N. by W., and we are on our proper course again. Waited for the moon to come up, so that we could see a bit before putting up mainsail and outer jib. Black as ink before that.

29th October.—Fresh gale blowing all day; very big seas coming down from the N.; ship rolling very badly. Nothing of special interest to report. Sailed through large quantities of Gulf weed. Considering the wind, we did not do at all well today. The last twenty-four hours have only put 143 miles to our credit.

30th October.—Wind still from N.E., but not quite so strong. During last night some very fierce gusts, with heavy rain. The mate had flying-fish for breakfast; several of them came aboard in the early morning,, and, as he was on watch, he bagged them. They have the appearance of a herring, but with fewer scales, and their wing fins are smaller than I expected. Quite a good day, though ship is still rolling very badly. Doc and I tried to play poker patience in the evening, but the cards wouldn't stay on the table, so we chucked it. Did 184 miles today, leaving about 780 to Bermudas. Should reach there about next Monday with luck. This engine must have a decent overhaul, and some new deck-hands are wanted. I don't fancy our foreigners where we are dealing with whisky and cash.

31st October.—Best day's run we have had yet—200 miles. Fair wind, strong to a fresh gale. If she doesn't do a good day's run just now in this weather, she will never do it. Engine had a tiff this evening about seven, and stopped. However, a drink of paraffin oil in the cylinders through the compression taps freed the pistons a bit, and she resumed duty at eleven.

The Doc spends a good deal of his time with the chief engineer when it is his watch. He acts as greaser—principally to avoid the skipper, I think, for ever since he helped the Old Man to put a 'Handy Billy' together he has not been popular. Unfortunately, he thought he was told to 'haul,' when the Old Man had said, "Leave the down-haul." Well, he hauled, and hauled the Old Man's thumb into a sheave. It was fairly dark at the time, so he got away! He is always, or nearly always, in the engineroom from eight till midnight. Last night the chief had a prank with him. He poured a little methylated spirit on one of the main bearing covers, then sent Doc to look at it with a slush lamp, in case it was heating. The subsequent conflagration nearly scared him stiff for a moment. Then we laughed. However, Doc has a sense of humour, and takes these things in good part. Wind has shifted to the S.E. and blowing a bit stronger. The next twenty-four hours should give us a good distance.

1st November.—Two months on this boat, and we are still a long way off our rendezvous, with expenses running up all the time. In fact, the worst part of the journey is still to come. Wind still blowing strongly from the S.E.

2nd November.—A most peculiar day. By all indications we should have had a dirty blow, but so far haven't, and, as the glass is beginning to rise, it doesn't look like it. About eight a very dirty-looking cloud came up from the west, along with a big swell. A good deal of lightning was flickering along the face of this cloud wall, and the glass was tumbling down. At 9:30 the S. E. wind we had had fell away to a calm The stage was set, but the play did not commence, for which everyone on board is thankful, for if we had a blow such as the skipper said was indicated at 9:30, Lord knows where it would blow us to. Ten o'clock arrived with torrential rain and thunder. Took in all sails and waited to see what would happen. The skipper and mate are at war properly. Mr. Mate got a telling off, and was nearly laid out, in fact. This has been brewing for some time. Mr. Mate has required a bit of a talking to. Very threatening till about six this evening, when it started to clear a bit. Glass still very low, but steady, and inclined to rise if anything. We had landed, the skipper said, between a S.E. gale and a W. gale; hence this pressure and swell. At 10 p.m. it was much clearer.

3rd November.—Saw what is known as a Portuguese man-of-war—or, in other words, a nautilus—last night. It is a jelly-fish-like thing, with several long streamers and a large fin on its back, which it can hoist up like a sail and move along the surface. At night it is a mass of phosphorescent light. Nothing much doing today. Big swell, and ship rolling damnably. We are all quite sore all over with just maintaining our balance. Much to our surprise, we have done 110 miles in the last twenty-four hours, and at 8 a.m. we were only 160 miles off Bermudas. Magnificent display of lightning all round us tonight. Barometer has been falling all day. Something very nasty has been taking place not very far away to cause this depression. Whatever it has been, we seem to have managed just to miss it— that is to say, if it is finished.

4th November.—I see. I say we have just managed to miss something. Well, I don't know quite what that was, but we have now missed something else, and I do know what that is. We have missed Bermudas. Yesterday we were twenty miles N.E. of the islands. Midday today we had made sufficient leeway to land us twenty-two miles to the south. Strong N.W. wind blowing. Saw a large steamer today—the first sign of life otherwise than ourselves for three weeks. Took all sails in at 9 p.m. Still making leeway.

5th November.—Up at six. Half gale, N.W. wind, rough sea. At midday we were twenty seven miles to the S., and going strong. Set all sails at 11 a.m. and stood off to N. by E. I don't see the slightest chance of making Bermudas in the next two days unless a complete change of wind takes place.

We had a curious experience last night. While beating up N. by E., we sighted the lights of what we thought was a large steamer not very far ahead and about two points to starboard. Kept our course, as the Old Man calculated she would be doing, anyhow, 10 knots, and by the time our leeway drifted us across her course she should be well astern of us. However, it didn't work out that way, for when we got near her we realized she was broken down and drifting before the wind. She showed no triangle of red lights, as she should have done. We were now too close to jibe to starboard, as the chances were we would have rammed her, and as the engine is not going, we can't tack to port. Everyone on deck gripped something and waited to see if our leeway or her drift would win. Her drift won, and we passed her stern about 40 ft. away. There is a very dirty sea running, so it's an almighty good thing we didn't touch. Weather better today. Still working to get N. of the islands and run down to them. We have now spent three days trying to get in, after being about fifteen miles off. Tacked ship, as machinery was going again. We are using our last bearing; no more spares.

CHAPTER XI

WE REACH BERMUDAS

8th November.—Got in at last. Tacked the ship early this morning and managed to creep to within eight miles of the islands. Fortunately the wind had changed a bit, and we got up to a short distance off and dropped anchor in twelve fathoms of water. Hope my windlass engine will work sufficiently well to bring the blooming thing up again.

9th November.—Got anchor up at 7:30 a.m. Engine worked beautifully. A pilot as black as your hand took us in through an entrance only about 40 yds. wide. A group of 365 islands and coral reefs makes up this place, which is full of wee lagoons, and would be a wonderful spot for a holiday with a motorboat or a big lug-sail.

Went ashore and got my cables off and did the Customs business. We are anchored just off a village with some warehouses and business offices dominated by a large hotel, but I haven't had time yet to examine the place properly. The boss should get here on Monday some time—that is, if he gets my cable. There are half a dozen bootlegging boats here at present. All bandy-looking craft, two-masted Nova Scotia schooners. One of them is at the wharf loading whisky at the moment. Doc and mate had words this morning. Mr. Mate wanted to get a case out of No. 1 hold for himself, and Doc, acting on my behalf, refused, and rightly. Raining heavily.

Several people arrived on board about 7:20 and told me how pleased they were to see us, and how much more pleased they would be if we placed a lot of orders with them. Went ashore with one of them and appointed our agents. The manager sent off my cables for me, and I had a wander round. A very quiet wee place. Bought some p.c.'s and a souvenir book. Arranged for an engineer to come off and quote for what must be done.

10th November.—Went ashore this morning to see if there was any answer to my cable. None yet; the boss is evidently away from home. Came aboard again and had some food. Decided to go and see some caves about five miles off. Chief engineer and I went ashore at 12:30 and tried to hire bicycles. I have very little money, so, as they asked 8s. for two hours, we decided to walk, and a very bonnie walk it was. Saw the most beautiful cave I have ever been in. A mass of stalactites, some of them 6 ft. in diameter, and anything up to 20 ft. to 30 ft. long, while others are as fine as a linen thread. The tide comes into part of it—the larger part. The water is about 40 ft. deep and as clear as crystal. Our guide told us that no life has ever been seen in the water. It was all lit up with electricity, and there must be about five hundred lights. Some of the stalactites are rose-coloured, some red, and some white, while all are reflected in the water. There are pontoons through that portion, with a wood pathway along them, so that to wander in and around the stalactites is like walking through a wood. They won't allow anyone to take photographs in the cave, and made me leave my camera at the entrance. There is a group of these caverns, one of which. is called 'Prospero's Cave,' and is supposed to be the scene of Shakespeare's *Tempest.* Prospero's is not so fine an example as some of the others, a lot of the stalactites being discoloured by the smoke from the guides' torches. It is not lit by electricity.

Got back to St. George's about 5:30, and had a dashed good dinner at Somer's Inn. Quite cheap; in fact, 6s. covered it. Got on board about eight. Had a whisky and turned in.

11th November.—They are celebrating Armistice Day ashore today, but not on board, where we were painting ship all day. I have had two cables. The boss will arrive on Friday. Had a motorboat trip in the afternoon with some fellows off a bootlegging trawler that is lying here. She is in trouble, the owner having disappeared with the money made up the coast. The men have not got their pay, and they can't find him. Very decent fellows. We all sailed over in a motorboat to Tom Moore's house, and had a beer, or perhaps two. Rather a quaint electrolier in one of the rooms—a ship's steering-wheel with the globes suspended from the spokes. It looked very well indeed. Got back about 3:30, and didn't go ashore again.

12th November.—Spent most of the day repacking the windlass, while the rest of the crew were painting ship. A lot of the men went ashore in the morning, some, as far as I have heard, doing their best to qualify for trouble.

The mate has managed to get himself hidden away on shore and hasn't put in an appearance since yesterday. I can see trouble looming ahead. Skipper has wind up and has lost all grip of his crew; in fact, I think he doesn't want to go on with this now, and isn't bothering his head really.

13th November.—Great night last night. I don't know what this bally ship will do next. About 11:30 p.m. last night it started to blow hard in big gusts, with heavy thunder and lightning. At midnight the lean Dutchman, who is acting watchman, thought sleeping a better way of spending the night than watching, so that he didn't notice we were dragging our anchor. It was only when our stern was about 50 yds. off the agent's wharf that the second mate happened to notice this in the glare of a flash of lightning. Wild excitement. By good luck our anchor fouled the mooring-chain of a buoy and brought us up a bit. We stopped when our stem was only 5ft. from the wharf, which we might easily have battered to bits, the coral rock of which it is built being so soft. The lightning was continuous by this time, and we could work as well as by day. Got her fixed with hawsers to various bollards on the wharf and waited till dawn. This morning the storm died away about six, and we had the luck to get a complete change of wind. The agent here, scenting a bit of profit to himself, came down, saw the Old Man, and generously offered the use of his tug to pull us back, a matter of about 200 to 300 yds., but, as his generosity required to be lubricated to the extent of £10, the offer was politely declined. We let the ship drift with the wind after we got our anchor up, and, using two buoys as brakes, about midday, we were back nearly to where we were before. I lifted a wire from one of the two buoys we had used, and hard work it was, getting seventy fathoms of heavy wire into a lifeboat. Messed about in a leaky boat doing this till the water was up to the thwarts; then came to the ship's side and bailed. I felt I needed a rest after this, so spent the balance of the day in a bos'n's chair slung over the stern repainting the ship's name in white and watching a swordfish that seemed to be keeping his eye on me. I don't know if they are dangerous or not, but, anyhow, was careful not to get into the water.

14th November.—Drove into Hamilton to meet the boss. The drive was beautiful, but very hot; there's no doubt these are lovely islands. Ship was four hours late. The boss was in a great state of excitement. Got back about five, and had dinner with him at the big hotel. Talked matters over. Had captain up, and chief engineer.

Got $200 to give to the crew. Mutiny has started, so there is a fine time ahead. Captain keeps clear of them, and stays in the charthouse, as he is fed up with the whole business. Some of the crew came aft and demanded a guarantee of a bonus, which I have no power to give them. Chased them forward. Drunken fights and rows all night. Doc and I spent it on No. 1 hatch, in case they tried broaching the cargo.

15th November.—The Scandehouvians spent most of the day sleeping and weaving plots to get at the cargo. I know I am going to be the object of any attacks, so I carry a useful belaying-pin. The two Glasgow lads gave me the wink that the crew are getting methylated spirit at 10*d.* a bottle. Awful stuff. I know they wouldn't try any nonsense when sober, but methylated spirit makes another man.

16th November.—Came up on deck about 7:30 a.m. this morning and found Doc gazing into space with a grin on his face. "Hullo, Doc! You look very pleased about something this morning. What's the joke?"

"Yes," he said, "bos'n's feeling better today, and told me a yarn about Peabody that's absolutely rich. You remember saying to me yesterday, 'What's the matter with him, that he never wants to go ashore now?'"

"Yes! I remember."

"Well, it appears that forward have been getting their methylated spirit through his ingenuity. You know that dog he brought on board in England?"

"Uh! Uh!"

"Now, the second day we were here he sold it to a nigger ashore for $5, which were invested in that muck for Hagersun, who has the wind up him. The next day he was on shore somewhere when he came across the dog. It ran after him. Some of his pals were waiting for him in a neighbouring dive, where he was due to do a step-dance (he's a beautiful step-dancer), and pass the hat round after. This is another method of replenishing the fo'c'sle purse. A coloured lad then took a fancy to the beast, and on this occasion $3 changed hands. The day before yesterday he was up at that football match, and, funnily enough, again picked up his late dog. Most of the population turn out to see these games. Our dog-fancier, when two irate coloured gentlemen descended on him and demanded the animal, was employing his time playing shoot for goal with an old tennis ball, using the animal and his jacket as goal-posts."

"And what happened then?"

"I understand," Doc said, "that his subsequent wanderings included most of this town, prior to his leaving hastily in a boat and coming on board. And that's, why I'm grinning, and why he stays on board, and, further, why he is hiding in my room at present, for Hagersun is down on him for refusing to go back to that dive and do more step-dances to allay his thirst."

17th November.—Men refused to turn to this morning unless they got a bonus guarantee. Defied the captain and got ashore. Had to do our own cooking. Cook stayed on board, but wouldn't work. Second mate unconscious. The foreign element came on board about eleven, attacked, and gave the cook another hammering. Peabody got hunted for his life and hid in my room, where I gave him his grub. This will come to shooting soon. Yacht *Star* came in— beautiful ship. Bootlegging, of course. She has just discharged 25,000 cases, and is on her way back to England. Hell of a night, howling, singing and fighting. Had the men down aft again. Captain off ashore, as he has heard of someone who is a keen draughts player. We shall have to get rid of all the Scandehouvians, including captain. I'm not going up the coast with that bunch on board. Chief engineer is fed up and wants to go, so we'll let him. From now on Glasgow will command in the oily regions, instead of London.

18th November.—Good lad, Peters! You've saved me a job. Hagersun can't see out of either of his eyes, and is confined to bunk, so to speak, as he has had the senses just about beaten out of him. Peters has stood this racket forward up till now, but when Hagersun went into the starboard side of the fo'c'sle about three this morning and, mistaking Peters's amiability for something else, grabbed him by the arm and called him a name no one will stand for, Hagersun got the surprise of his young life, for he was sent flying, and a very wrathful Glasgow sailor dragged him out to the deck and socked him proper, while Morrison saw that the two Finns did not interfere. Wish I had seen it.

19th to 23rd November.—Same sort of thing, no work being done and men mutinous. The boss has arranged to ship them off by the *Star*, so we shall pay off tomorrow. I am carrying a revolver now. Captain wouldn't go near the fo'c'sle to warn them to pack up without Doc and self coming with him.

24th November.—Paid off the whole foreign crowd, including the captain, Peabody and the chief engineer. The mate turned up at the shipping office, his first appearance since the third day of our arrival. Don't know where he has been, and, judging by his looks, I don't think he does either. So he is off home also. Mr. Lean Dutchman has disappeared altogether, so he is marked down in the official log as 'Deserted ship.'

Have engaged a new man. The boss is looking after the others. This blessed skipper had the cheek to tell him I wasn't to be trusted, and he had better put someone to watch me. I am captain at present. This is hellish all the same, apart from the worry, for the Lord knows when we shall get our job of work done.

I am writing this on the 28th of November, and I'm bothered if I can remember from day to day what we did. All I know is, I was a damned sight too tired at night to do anything but turn in. Spent one day in Hamilton with the new captain, looking for a crew. Found a second engineer and booked him—a Scot; good fellow, I think. Another journey to Hamilton later on with the new chief looking for more oil. Got some. Interviewed some Bermudians one day who want to come with us—a likely-looking crowd except one, who is a nigger. Later on signed on four of them as A.B.'s. The new captain's son, a youngster of nineteen, comes as second mate. Got a mate and a cook another day. Hope he is a decent one.

29th November.—I think this ship is mad or something. We have spent the last two days trying to get the engine started up properly. Everything has gone wrong. The fuel pumps were all out of adjustment, I think on purpose; she blows joints with great ease and dexterity, and today, when the boss insisted on her going out of the harbour, she blew three joints and then nearly laid the Doc out by blowing a red-hot ignition stud, which just missed him, out of the cylinder bulb. We were under way, and approaching the narrows, so now we are anchored in the fairway, and waiting till about seven tomorrow for a tug to take us outside.

CHAPTER XII

OFF AGAIN

30th November.—By the by, we have got a young pig on board. This is for our Christmas dinner, so he has twenty-six days to fatten himself up in, and I hope he is successful. Tug arrived about 6:30 and disturbed us in our slumbers. Fortunately Dick (Mr. Ping Pong) had been up a bit earlier and got the donkey-boiler going, with plenty of pressure to raise the anchor. Wind almost favourable. Getting along about 2 to 3 knots. Worked in the engineroom all day. Had a turn at the concertina. I woke up St. George's on two occasions with the bagpipes, and the only Scot living there promptly stole a boat and came out to listen, although, as I heard afterwards, he was waiting outside the church for his girl. He must have kept her waiting about half an hour.

By midnight we had Gibbs Hill Light well down astern.

1st December.—Worked all forenoon at the engine, and got her going about one. Running well too. Think she should be all right now. Kept her on till six. What a difference on board this ship now! Peace and quiet reign where strife and discord were before. The new captain doesn't believe in progressive games with the sails, thank goodness. Bos'n has now sobered up and is working. He has made a dodger for the bridge, which makes it a much more comfortable place to be on. As we near the cold weather, it will be a blessing to the man at the wheel and whoever is on watch. So far the ocean is peaceable. I hope it intends to keep this up. Cheery is the new second engineer's name, and it fits his nature. He is a good yarner. I have just given the pair of them half a bottle, and will join them shortly with the other half.

2nd December.—Engines not quite satisfactory yet. Fine day. Wind, however, not favourable. We are at present heading in for Cape Hatteras, very much south of our destination. Got engine going again about two. Will keep it running now unless it stops of its own accord. Spent evening studying the art of navigation, as neither of the new mates can use a sextant or know anything of ex-meridians or prime verticals. Fortunately our late skipper showed me how to use the sextant and explained how to find longitude by chronometer. Captain Lecky is doing the rest.

3rd December.—Cut my own hair again to day, very successful. Fine day. Tacked ship about 11 a.m., and so off on a course about N.E. We don't want to get too close to Hatteras. Our pig is getting quite friendly, and will come to you if you call. Will be sorry to see it killed. Nothing much doing all day.

4th December.—I have made a proper bunk for myself now that the captain sleeps in my old one. Very comfortable, narrow enough to prevent my rolling about. It is the saloon settee with a board along the front. Finished my whisky book this forenoon. Weather showing signs of getting colder. We should be in the Gulf Stream this time tomorrow. It is about two hundred miles wide about here. Mess-boy got a dolphin yesterday, with a line over the stern and a hook baited with a piece of white rag. A very pretty fish, about 12 lbs. weight. While dying, its body changed from red, orange and blue to a dirty grey. We had it for breakfast and it was very good. I hear we should get plenty of cod off New York. There is a reasonable chance of getting there soon now, if 'Hughie,' the engine, doesn't let us down.

Damn! A goodly portion of the fresh meat we took on board at Bermuda has gone bad already. However, we have managed to save some of it. We are about 280 miles on our way.

CHAPTER XIII

RUM ROW

5th December.—Started off the day doing better speed than we have done yet. Bent an extra rope to the gaff guys and let the sails well out. Blowing strongly from S., and we are making about 7 knots most of the day. About four in the afternoon it came on to blow hard and began to look very dirty, and by eight in the evening it was blowing a gale and the glass had dropped to 29.4.

Shortly after midnight the foresail gaff snapped and the sail was badly torn in a dozen places. The loose end of the gaff managed to get stuck up in the lee rigging, and we had the very dickens of a job getting it down, as by this time the wind was strong enough to have blown one off the ratlines had anyone attempted the outboard side. As it was, the pressure of some gusts jammed one tight against them. It was nearly pitch dark, which didn't make the job easier. All this time the *Cask* was taking it well over the hatches, and, with the water swirling more than waist high, the old rule of 'one hand for the ship and one for oneself' was a deep necessity. I was winding the throat down-haul round the barrel of a winch when something washed past me. It was our pig. I yelled as loud as I could, and by luck there was a slight lull in the racket and bos'n heard. I could just see him make a wild dive, then he and our Christmas dinner came up together against the bridge bulkhead, both spitting sea water. He grasped the iron ladder that leads to the bridge, and held on till there was a little less water to get through before hauling piggie by a hind leg to the fo'c'sle, where he was finally locked in the crew's W.C.

It took about two hours to get that gaff down and the remains of the sail tied up on the boom. About half an hour later I was sheltering with mate in the lee of the chart-house when Cap came round and shouted, "This wind is still hardening. Call all hands and get the mainsail down. It won't stand any more." "Aye, sir." Hardly were those words said when a wicked squall hit us, flattening the sea, and about eight feet deep of solid spindrift from the wave-tops screamed over us. Away went the mainsail, torn from the wire leech. We had another picnic getting that housed. In the same squall the outer jib tore loose from the gaskets and disappeared into the spindrift. "We can do nothing with her till this takes off a bit," skipper said. So I suggested we should have a stiff tot all round and make ourselves as comfortable below as possible. Served out a tot of rum to all hands, lashed the wheel, then went below, where I got out of my soaking things and into my bunk. This was about four in the morning. Luckily, the Gulf Stream is nearly tepid here, so it wasn't cold.

The ship is hardly doing any rolling. Wind much too fierce to permit of a sea getting up.

6th December.—Had a sleep for a couple of hours; when I woke day had arrived, so got up to go and have a look. Cap, whose room opens off the saloon, heard me, and shouted, "Don't think from the noise it's any easier, Mr. Mac What's the glass doing?" Looked at the glass in the saloon. "Twenty-eight point five," I shouted back. At ten last night it was 29. Hub! never saw a glass do this before. The pointer was moving slowly back and forward through an arc of 1/10 inch. I don't know what that foretells, nor does Cap.

Put on an oilskin and went up to look. Opened the companion door, and as I stepped out the wind got me, and, before I realized what was doing, I found myself in a heap against the taffrail. Got hold of the top strake and hauled myself to my feet. It was a sight I shan't forget. I couldn't see the surface of the sea through the smoke in any direction. Looking, forward to the bridge, the after-hatch was almost hidden by the spray blown horizon tally across it. It was as though something unending and almost solid was rushing, roaring and screaming past us. Facing it, breathing was impossible. The weight of wind was almost visible. It needed no imagination to visualise a nebulous entity, endowed with infinite mass and energy, always coming and always fading, booming and crying into the water-rent distance.

Hell! Hailstones now, like bullets. When they arrived I made for the companion via a bollard that was a refuge halfway, and got down below with no further loss of time.

Well, Mr. Mac, what's it like?

"Like nothing on earth I've ever seen before," I replied.

"It's one of the hardest winds I've ever seen," Cap said. "I had a look when you jammed up against the rail, but I don't think it will last much longer, certainly not like what's going on now."

Got back into my bunk again and lay and listened to it. About 10 a.m. glass had risen and the wind had eased off sufficiently to let the sea get up, so we are rolling again.

7th December.—No cooking today. The bulkhead door of the galley had somehow worked open and the fire got drowned out properly. Very uncomfortable all day, but weather easing all the time. Wind suddenly shifted into north in the late afternoon, so we put up the inner jib and spanker to try to steady her a bit. Worked at the engine most of the night, and got it going again at 2 p.m. the following day; and as I write, at 9 p.m., it is still attending to its business. Well, our storm damage has amounted to an outer jib gone, foresail ruined, mainsail badly damaged but repairable, and a broken gaff, which I don't know how we can replace. A ring holding one of the peak blocks to the mast gave way, and that started the mainsail going.

Spent most of this day cleaning up storm damage in the holds and storeroom and getting coal up from No. 1 hold. Wind still dead ahead, but fallen sufficiently to enable the engine to give us about 3 knots. We are out of the Gulf Stream now and it is decidedly colder. I shall have to think of underclothing tomorrow or the next day. Cook is laid up, so the cooking is suffering. That pig is an amusing beast; he appears thoroughly to enjoy being washed about by the seas coming aboard, and gets tied up in ropes and in between people's legs. He landed Peters on his back this afternoon while he was struggling along with a load of coal. Much to Peters' annoyance, and also to Mr. Pig's when he found himself bombarded with lumps of it for his pains. Difficult to write; rolling very heavily.

9th December.—Fine day. Good sailing breeze from S. W. again. Nothing out of the ordinary to write about. At noon we were about

210 miles off our rendezvous. Pig was sick and inclined to be vicious. Cook back at work, I am glad to say.

Took main half of gaff off the foremast and had another look at the sail. Beyond repair. A certain amount of dry rot in the gaff. At 4:30 p.m. heaved the lead, as we ought now to be in soundings, but found no bottom—hand lead-line only 40 fathoms.

Tried again at 7:30 p.m. and found 33 fathoms. At 8:30 p.m. anchored in 28 fathoms, so we are now practically at our journey's end. Have given the chief engineer a bottle. He, the second, and the are holding high revel in his cabin. Did some fishing over the side. Got one nice codling. There should be plenty of fish, I think. So as long as our fresh water holds out we shall be in clover. 'Cold clover.' Warmer here than I expected. Have not yet put on flannels. Served out the firearms and twelve rounds each, so we are ready as far as that is concerned. Captain, mates, engineers, Doc and self with revolvers. The rifle, with ten rounds, is to be kept on the bridge for the use of the man on watch while we are unloading.

10th December.—We got a lot of fish last night, and had most excellent cod for breakfast this morning. Dull and misty. Estimate we are at present 25 to 26 miles off land, and are waiting steam in the donkey to get up anchor and creep in and find our proper place. Got anchor up at 9:30. The windlass wouldn't work, and the old familiar cry echoed through the ship, "Where's Mr. Mac?" So I had to go on the fo'c'sle head and heave up 75 fathoms, which took a little time. Have gone in about ten miles and can just see land, though what part of America it is we shan't exactly know until we can manage to identify some of the lights after dark. Have got the stove in the saloon going well after some trouble, and it is quite warm and comfortable. It is a pity the anchor has got to come up again, but I trust it will be for the last time until the cargo is discharged. Raised the anchor again at 7:30 p.m., and motored up a few more miles till we were S.E. of Ambrose Light (which we have now identified). Had a deuce of a job getting one of the shackles over the gipsy wheel on the windlass, as it kept jumping back. Got it over by means of a messenger from No. 1 winch. Glands leaking badly, so had to work in a cloud of steam. Did a bit of fishing, and got one small codling, about 4 lbs., I should say. Turned in at eleven.

11th December.—Got up at 3 a.m. and knocked about until about five, when I turned in again. Raining and cold in the early morning. Cleared about seven, when wind shifted into the N. and didn't get any warmer. Spent part of the forenoon fishing, but got nothing but large dog-fish. Tied one of them to an empty bottle and let him float astern, using him as a target for some revolver practice. Got him with the second shot at about ten yards. Not bad in a rough sea. Second mate and I have a competition with the mate and one of the sailors as to who will catch the most fish in a week. A bottle of whisky is to be the prize. So far Mr. Mate is winning. Got more coal up in the afternoon and did some more fishing; no luck, though. So far no customers have arrived to purchase whisky. It was too rough most of to-day any how, but I had expected somebody out to have a look at us. I believe last night a boat did come round us, but it did not hail, and went back. I wish we could get started. I want to have a sight of these gentry and their methods of working. There are several more ships lying about four miles from us, nearer the Long Island shore. When this wind moderates we shall move up in line with them.

12th December.—Beautiful morning, but a little cold. Northerly wind. Got anchor up at nine and sailed up to within a mile or so of a steamer. The bay here forms roughly two sides of a square, and we are lying fifteen miles off each side. This should be our permanent place, I think. Fell flat calm, and we had excellent hopes of customers or at least a visit from the boss, but nothing doing. Did some fishing, but got nothing but dog-fish, which we executed in various ways, such as nailing them to bits of wood, etc. About 8:30 a Revenue launch came round and had a look at us, but did not hail or pay any outward attention beyond trying to read the name on our stern. Turned in at 9:30 p.m.

13th December.—Turned out again at midnight and stood watch till 4 a.m. All officers are standing watch; it works out at four hours every second night. Made tea twice and paced the bridge in a business-like manner till I was relieved by the second mate. Slept fitfully till 7:30 a.m. At 11:30 a.m. an aeroplane came over and inspected us carefully; may have been sent by His Nibs. Half a gale of wind blowing. Heavy sea coming in from the Atlantic; the ship is bucking to her anchor like a fresh horse tied to a lamppost. We have 140 fathoms of chain out on one anchor, and the other with about fifteen fathoms on the bottom, ready in case we drag. So far we haven't, I'm glad to say. Captain and mess-boy had some private conversation today, as he was found flourishing the second engineer's loaded revolver, which he took from his room. I have no watch tonight, so will have, I hope, a good sleep.

14th December.—Damnable night. At midnight wind increased to something more than a gale, and fairly screamed round us. Captain and self got up and had a walk round. At one, shifted suddenly into N.W., and left us rolling in the trough of a dickens of a sea. Everything in the galley poured out and clattered about, shipping seas from side to side. At 3 a.m. fall of snow. Very cold all day. Spent most of the day in the saloon with a good fire on. Had a religious argument with the second engineer for about an hour this evening. Captain, ably assisted by myself, on the rampage about the cook's baking of bread. More flour is being wasted than used. Turned in at 10 p.m.

15th December.—Turned out again at 3:45 for my vigil on deck. Damned cold, ten degrees of frost, but fortunately little wind now. Made some tea and put in time walking about and yarning with Peters. At 7 a.m. lit the stove in the saloon and had another cup of tea. Spent morning getting coal, beef, pork, etc., up out of No. 1 hold. At two captain decided to move up nearer the shore. When we hove in the port chain we found the anchor had vanished. Must have broken off during the blow the night before last. Had a deuce of a job bending one of our spare ones. The swivelling flukes had frozen in, and it wasn't until we had lit a fire under it and hammered the flukes with a fore- hammer that we got it free. It was a job to get it overboard after shackling it on, but we managed it. About 5 p.m. a boat came along and asked for me, saying they would return later and give us our station, whatever they may mean by that; also that a Revenue boat was coming later also. The Revenue boat duly put in an appearance, came close up and took our photograph—nice of them, but I don't suppose we shall get a copy. Played cards

for a bit in the evening. Looking very like snow and a good deal of
it. Highest glass today we have had so far this trip—30.4, which is
very high for this time of the year. Bos'n in a great funk; some one
has been spinning him a yarn about American jails. Some of the rest
of today may require to be written tomorrow. Today still has some
hours to run, but I am tired and going to turn in.

16th December.—Nothing required to be written extra. Slept the
sleep of the just until 7:15. Fine day, nothing particular doing during forenoon. Hellish salt soup for dinner. At 2:40 a boat was sighted coming out. Same boat as yesterday. The sea was fairly rough
and it had a job getting alongside us. One of them came on board
with letters and papers—New York papers and letters from the 'high
hied 'un.' Good news at last. Our station is fixed four miles S. S. E.
the Fire Island lightship, and we are to proceed there as quickly as
possible. Got up anchor at 3:15. By the by, an aeroplane arrived
alongside while the fellow off the motorboat was in the cabin. He
got off at once in case it might be hostile, but it can't have been, for
he dropped a message in the water which they picked up. It was
not for us, however. Strong S.W. wind helped us to our new station,
seventeen miles off. Did 6-1/4 knots. Dropped anchor at seven.
Fairly heavy sea running and we are rolling heavily. Could probably have been discharging tonight had the weather been suitable. I
am on watch from eight till twelve tonight. Not cold despite strong
wind. Charthouse nice and comfortable. Have a paraffin stove burn-
ing in it, though there's not much time to sit inside in case ship
wants to leave another anchor on the bottom. Time is just up, so I'll
disturb the mate in his slumbers, have a cup of tea, and turn in.
Hope tomorrow is calm and we get some work done. I am busy
growing a beard at present, and am a filthy-looking object.

Several things happened, however, before I got the mate disturbed. Firstly, a heavy rope fender that was over the side threatened to carry away and had to be hauled on board. It was the deuce
of a weight, and, with occasional seas arriving over the gunwale, it
required a certain amount of care. The next trouble was the 'C class'
lifeboat, which is perched up on No. 1 hatch, and started to come
off the chocks. Nice job getting that fixed. Then I was looking over
the bridge dodger forward and saw something come charging aft in

a sea. Thought the pig was in for it that time, but when the object brought up against the galley bulkhead with a crash that shook the bridge I realized it was something heavier than live pig. Went to see, and found it was dead pig in the shape of a 360 lb. barrel of salt pork, so had to get that lashed up. Morrison was on watch with me, so we had a busy time. Nothing much doing today, as the sea is too strong for boats to come out. Just messed about and did odd jobs.

U.S. REVENUE CUTTER *SENECA*

A SPEEDBOAT LEAVING WITH 50 CASES

CHAPTER XIV

FIRST ORDERS

18th December.—This day has been a little more like the thing. Did some odd jobs about the ship in the morning and ate heartily at twelve of stew and prunes. Mate prophesied the first boat would come off to us at 2:30, but at 1:30 the cry went up that a boat was coming. It brought a man called Hamman, who, with his partner, is supposed to have bought the cargo. They are paying for it on shore at the rate of $21 and send us orders for all they get. I am at liberty to sell to anyone, but at $23 one dollar is to be credited to Hamman & Co. This is apparently part of our fee which we have to pay for protection. Exactly what we are being protected against I don't yet know. These people have their own protection to pay for ashore, *i.e.*, the State police, Coast Guard, etc., and their only fear is, apparently, of the flying squads of Federal Police, who don't stay long enough in one place to be got at. It's a most amazing situation. There must be over 200,000 cases of whisky within a few miles of here waiting to go ashore.

It appears we are in the wrong place, so up anchor and steam off E. again about five miles. We are now in the rum circle off Fire Island inlet and 8-1/2 miles off shore. No sooner had our anchor gone down than a boat came for 200 cases. This was an order from the boss, so there's no money in the safe yet. Splendid. Handed over the cases, and away went our friends as pleased as Punch. They could have taken 400, but had not the necessary order or the cash. Had just sat down to tea at six, when two other boats came along. Took the captains to the cabin and started bargaining. Damn! shout of Revenue cutter. Up on deck like scared hares, cutter away in the distance. One man is on the bridge to keep a look-out. One of the boats was leaking badly, and the crew were going to dump with us 100 cases they had previously got from another ship, but changed their minds and made off. The other one had 13 cases he had found floating about, and he left them with us and went off to look after his pal in case he got into trouble. One boat today had to throw overboard 300 cases to escape arrest. This fellow had found some of that. No more excitement. Am on watch from twelve to four, so am turning in for an hour's sleep.

19th December.—Busy day today. The boss came out and generally messed about. Brought no mail, all the same; he had left it in Atlantic City for some reason best known to himself. First boat came out at 7:30 a.m., and from that time on we were at it hard all day nearly, with scarcely time to eat. By evening we had got rid of 1,400 cases. Not a bad day's work. Wrote home reporting progress. Several forward very drunk tonight. They will require to be spoken to severely. No Revenue cutters worried us today. Beautiful day, quite warm. Wind got up a little in the evening. One boat came off at 8 p.m., but it was too rough to transfer stuff. The boat fellows appear very decent chaps as a whole, but everything doesn't show on the surface. Feeling a bit tired.

20th December.—Another busy day. Cutters round in the forenoon, so got coal up and holds straightened out a bit. Cutter went off to E. about midday, and the rest of the day was busy, for we sold just over 1,000 cases in five hours. Captain read the Riot Act to our drunks, and they all affirm their conversion to the principles of teetotalism—for a while. I can see myself getting damned little sleep with this Yank on board, as he wants to sit up to all hours and won't get up in the morning. I am on watch, for instance, from 4 a.m. to 8 tomorrow, and he is still talking at midnight. He was for a while a New York detective. Hell of a job tonight getting my books square; still $100 out. $31,760 in the safe already.

21st December.—Up at 3.45 a.m. Quite warm, in fact the weather is astonishing for this season. Divided my time between looking for my $100 and pacing the bridge. Very dull and misty; there's not much chance of getting a lot of business done today, I am afraid. Spent forenoon getting cargo up on deck and raised about 1,000 cases to be ready for anyone coming. A few boats arrived in the afternoon—five all told; they took 383 cases. Not much for a whole day. The holds are beginning to show signs of getting down a good bit now. Donkey-man got very merry and bright tonight, so much so that the captain got handcuffs out and was nearly putting him in irons. Don't know what took him. He is a good sort, and I got quite a lot of information as to what the foreign elements were up to. He can't read or write English, and has a white wife in England whom he is very fond of. When mails arrive out I have often the job of reading his letters for him, and also writing his replies, to which he puts a queer mark at the end.

Caught five ling over the stern, so thank goodness we shall have some fresh fish for breakfast tomorrow. I thought I should get to bed about ten, but fell into a discussion on astronomy which lasted till twelve midnight Feeling very tired.

22nd December.—Dull again today, with S.E. wind and occasional rain. The first excitement of the day was killing our friend the pig. The mate, who is a butcher, in private life, took that matter in hand, and an expeditious job he made of it—killing, cleaning and hanging in about thirty-five minutes. Just as he finished a cry went up, "Boats arriving." Not much doing in the way of business. Only about 400 cases over the side.

CHAPTER XV

A CHRISTMAS BLOW

23rd December.—Again an unprofitable day as far as business is concerned. We feel a little in the dumps, for, when the first of our own people's boats came out, they told us that the night before last eight of the fellows that had been out to us in two different boats had gone west. On their way ashore it got up very nasty, and, as they were shipping so much water, they had to jettison the cargo. Even with that, one of the boats sank. The four on board managed to get on to the other boat with great difficulty. Unfortunately their adventure didn't end with that, for they picked three men off still another boat that had broken down. It was pitch dark by this time, and there was a very difficult bar to cross. The steersman says he doesn't know exactly what happened, but remembers the boat yawing wildly on the top of a big wave, and then, as it sank in the trough, there was a terrible bump when the keel hit the top of the bar. The subsequent lurch threw ten of them overboard and drowned them. They were all very decent fellows, the best we have come across so far. It was dashed hard luck on them, when they had practically reached safety. The steersman, the only survivor, says they could have ridden it out until the tide had risen sufficiently to make the bar safe, if one of the Revenue cutters hadn't been running about near shore. The Revenue cutters are very active in shore at present. Yesterday morning saw a motorboat captured. Don't understand it as the day was clear and the boat, I should think, must have seen the cutter at least a mile off. Anyhow, he steered straight into her, and, when he was about four hundred yards off, he had the 'Clammy Hughie' put on him. The boss visited us today, and brought letters, I am glad to say, but he didn't stay long on board. We have got a little fresh meat now, and it is a pleasant change from salt pork. Only two boats for stuff today, and they took 125 cases off. Ship is rolling very badly, so that the cases we have on deck in piles are wandering about a bit and will require to be watched. Glass going down steadily.

24th December.—Strong N.W. wind, with no possibility of any boats being able to get alongside. It was cold, with a little snow, in the morning. Had a sleep in the afternoon. Captain spent it showing cook how to bake bread. He has also made the Christmas pudding, which is to be cooked tonight. That pig is very tender, so the joint tomorrow ought to be good. The *Aquitania* passed about four hundred yards from us this morning, bound for New York. I think my old pal Jack Buchanan is on board. I know from local papers that 'Chariot's' Company are due across by her, anyhow. Took two photographs of her, but am afraid the light will not be good enough. My beard is getting quite good, and looks less like a dirty mark on my chin. Am on watch twelve to four, so am going to have a sleep.

25th December.—Christmas Day. What a way to spend a Christmas! It certainly is a method I don't think I shall repeat. Got up, or, rather, as I was still up, put some warm things on and went on watch at midnight. Bridge was pretty cold, but there was a good fug in the chart house. Came off at four and called the second mate, after which I turned in and slept well. Breakfasted at 8:30. We should have had what the mate caught, but at the last moment bacon and eggs were substituted. We live on the fat of the land as long as boats come, for they sell us stores. Nothing doing all forenoon. Captain had made the Christmas pudding, but unfortunately it had had an accident and stuck to the bottom of the pot. Dinner consisted of tomato soup, roast pork with preserved potatoes, and the captain's pudding. For drink, whisky and port wine. Quite a good dinner, which we all enjoyed very much, except the second engineer, who is not a lover of pork as fed on board a semi-sailing ship! Felt rather sleepy after all that, so lay down about 2:15 and slept steadily until five, when we adjourned for tea. Pretty rough all day. At the time of writing—6 p.m.—the wind is increasing, and it looks rather like a stormy night. Wind S.W., but not so cold. Nothing specially interesting to report today.

26th December.—Nothing doing today as far as business is concerned, as it was much too stormy for small boats to come alongside. Spent most of the day stacking stuff on deck and getting some more out of the hold. I can see some damage being done directly we get a big roll on, but my orders are to have 100 cases of each brand on deck; "and don't argue with me." Played a game called 'five hundred' at cards, captain and I against the second mate and mate. We lost badly. It was a sort of mixture of bridge, auction bridge and poker—quite a good game. Bos'n again on the verge of D.T.; in fact, he is pointing out things to us that are walking up and down the bulkhead at the foot of his bunk. I can see him cashing his checks one of these days. I am on watch from four to eight tomorrow morning, so good night.

27th December.—This has been a varied kind of a day, from the point of view both of weather and interest. Got up at four and had some tea. Did a little fishing and got three nice ling. The cutter *Gresham*, which had been circling round the group of boats lying here—six including ourselves—came to anchor at 7 a.m. in the middle of us, so that put a stop to business for the forenoon. However, he went off at 1:15 p.m. in the direction of New York. Utilised that time to square up the holds and get some more on deck. Odd boats came off during the afternoon and relieved us of some stuff. One fellow brought the news that the boat the boss and some of Hamman & Co. were in on Sunday broke down, and had to signal to the Revenue cutter for assistance, with the result that they were both taken into New York to explain what they were doing out here. The New York papers have a full account of this, and further state that the boss was in possession of $46,000. I don't know what to make of it. They may deport him. It may be serious or it may not.

Glass dropping and wind into S.E. One boat came out for 295 cases, but had to bolt as the cutter came in sight, at least its lights did. They left two of their crew on board, so we entertained them to tea. At this time they still had to receive 118 cases. I didn't think they would get back as the wind was rising, and I wasn't looking forward to having perhaps to entertain these blighters for several days; however, their pals returned and got off their marooned friends and the balance of their order in good condition. Our day's sales amounted to 518 cases—not bad, seeing the cutter was out all morning. At mid night it is blowing hard from the S.E. and looks like a dirty night. That means a deuce of a swell tomorrow.

28th December.—I . . . I . . . what the translation of the first two words of this sentence is I don't know now, as the engine, at the time I was attempting to write, was making so much vibration that that is the result. Devil of a day today. Strong gale. In the morning found cases smashed up all over the decks; can't say how many, but should think at least sixty. Repacked them all forward near the fo'c'sle and jammed them up between hatch coamings as tightly as possible. Two hours later, cases all over the place again and a lot more smashed up. Wind very fresh. During tea felt a funny tremor run through the ship. Went up to the fo'c'sle head and found that either we had broken another cable or that the ship was dragging, as we were broadside to the seas. Dropped the port anchor and let out seventy fathoms of chain gradually. That brought her head up and stopped her. Very much afraid the anchor is gone; if so, that means the end at present, as we shall require to shift out of this tomorrow. Ship rolling very heavily, and foremast getting looser every day. On watch eight till twelve. At 11:30 starboard chain hanging up and down.

29th December.—Terrible mess on deck this morning. A lot more cases had been smashed up and broken bottles were everywhere. At nine, got up the starboard chain, but there was no anchor on it. Well, that finishes it. In 'military parlance,' the situation is that on the port side we have 110 fathoms of chain and one anchor, on the starboard about thirty fathoms of chain and no anchor, our other spare being a light kedge. A factor that affects the situation is that some of the links on the port chain have opened over one eighth of an inch, so that a heavy blow will do them in. If the blow is from the S.E. we shall all be on the beach, as the old *Cask* couldn't get out of this *cul-de-sac* in the teeth of a strong gale from the Atlantic. No Federal jails or deportation as a D.B.S. for this chicken, if it can be avoided. Anyhow, I understand our insurance policy is void inside American territorial waters.

Started in to put the unbroken cases back into the holds. Got that done about twelve, as the wind luckily shifted into N.W. We got anchor up at two, and started off on our travels again, back to Bermuda. I suggested we might fly a signal to the other schooners in case any of the boats enquired for us, so we hoisted a display of bunting which, when translated, meant "Proceeding Bermuda report only one anchor left." Passed quite close to one ship, and, from all the notice he took of our bunting, he must have thought we were merely trying to be impertinent to him, so I am afraid the first news the boss will get of us is when I cable from Bermuda—that is to say if he is not in jail. Our troubles started early; hadn't gone a mile running before a fine N.W. breeze when bang went the gaff of the mainsail. The bolt holding it to the slide on the mast had sheared. Got it down after a lot of trouble, fixed a shackle in its place, and hoisted the sail again. We have our American friend with us. Couldn't put him ashore, and cannot risk waiting for a boat in case a sou'-easter turns up, and sou'-easters are the rule at this season. He is not at all pleased about it, and calls it being shanghaied. But he has turned out a first-rate fellow, so we shall do our best for him as far as Bermuda. At six the shackle we had put on the main gaff burst and left the end of the gaff sticking up in the rigging. It was too dark to work at it, so we had to leave it till tomorrow. Ship travelling fast before a half-gale N.W. wind. Turned in about 11 p.m.

30th December.—Got gaff under control and fixed him up again, this time with six shackles, so will see if that will do any good. Making good progress again today before a strong W. wind. Poor Hamman is not a sailor and is not enjoying himself one little bit. Thinks we must have tough stomachs to put up with it. Gaff carried away again, so captain has housed the sail as useless to us. Not much doing during the rest of the day. Cooking very bad just now. Have finished our better provisions, such as tinned salmon, etc.

31st December.—Chief engineer and I had a look at the runway on the main mast this morning, and decided if we cut away about 6 ins. of it above the boom, we would manage to use the slide off the broken fore-gaff. No sooner thought than done. It was hard work chipping through tough steel to that extent, balancing on the boom with the ship rolling badly, but we did it in two hours and a half. Still the troubles pile on. Found the mizzen-boom was badly cracked and bent. That's going to go next. Turned in at ten, intending to be up at twelve for first footing purposes.

1st January.—Didn't wake till two. However, got a bottle and visited the fo'c'sle, wished them all the best. Bos'n far from better, and still inclined to see things that are not there. Next visit was the Doc's room. Found him, the mate and chief engineer very confidential. Went and pulled second engineer out, and we joined the other three. Second mate supposed to be on watch, but he blew in as well. Proceedings were rather abruptly terminated, however. Second engineer and self were sitting on the Doc's bunk with an open port above our heads, when a big sea struck the ship's side as she suddenly lay over and it poured in on us. Thought it wasn't going to stop coming through. Left about a foot of water on the floor, and of course soaked the bed through. This was owing to the steersman going to the fo'c'sle for a drink. After that I retired and got into my bed on the settee. Weather worse, heavy gale blowing, big seas. Hamman is scared out of his wits and thinks he is going to be drowned. Very heavy rain and wind squall struck us at three in the afternoon and broke mizzen-boom. The extraordinary thing was that at the worst of the squall the wind suddenly shifted about three points and then ceased. No more for about five minutes, and then it seemed to blow vertically down on us so that the ship lost all way and nearly rolled over.

This lasted about ten minutes. Cooking is getting worse and worse. It has been a very fine New Year's Day!

2nd January.—Strong wind and big sea all day. No sun, so we were unable to get any sights. Knocked a rise out of the Doc in the evening, while he was taking watch in the engineroom and had the job of oiling. Dropped some steel hanks on the end of a string down the ventilator, and had him running about to see where the noise was. Don't quite know where we are.

3rd January.—Not much doing. No sights worth anything. Weather moderating considerably. Captain thinks we are not many miles off. At 8 p.m. the mate sighted Gibbs Hill Light from the mast-head. Our first captain told me on several occasions he had known men who had what he called 'seagull instinct.' I realized today what he meant, for since leaving the American coast we haven't had a sight of the sun, yet here we are striking a small group of islands seven hundred miles away to within an hour or two. And that in a ship that makes leeway a fine art. There's more than just dead reckoning in it. The Old Man must have just that 'seagull instinct.' More power to him!

CHAPTER XVI

HAMILTON

4th January.—Stayed up most of the night and messed about. Burnt two blue lights to warn the pilot, who came aboard at 7:15 a.m. and took us round to Hamilton. Went ashore, cabled Mr. Cork at home, and sent a letter to the boss via a circuitous route in case the authorities are watching his mail-bag. Captain entered his protest. Came back to ship at 5:30. All ashore, so had to make my own tea. Bos'n having a private spree. Wrote up ship's accounts till turning in at 10:30. The other officers have gone to a dance.

5th January.—Quite a varied day today. Skipper and I had our survey along with Lloyd's man, who came on board at nine, and after finishing our business at the Customs we hired a carriage and went off to St. George's to look for anchors and cables, also to order a new foresail and jib. Had my first decent meal for a month at Somer's Inn. No anchors or cables were to be obtained. Saw the collier that was in Funchal at the same time as Ourselves: she was having a new blade put on her propeller. Came back to Hamilton and spent the evening with Hamman, our shanghaied friend. Excellent dinner, with turtle steak—which I tasted for the first time; very good. Hamman has a double room with a bathroom attached, so I slept there, and had my first decent hot bath since 27th September. By gum, I needed it! Got into bed at 1:30.

6th January.—Sunday, went down to the wharf at ten, and found Peters and the mess-boy there with the ship's boat. Strong wind was blowing, and we had a deuce of a job getting out. Spent the rest of the day writing and taking it easy in the hotel, at least until six, when we—that is, Doc, Hamman and self—went round to the captain's house. Had rather a varied and peculiar evening, but very enjoyable, as the Old Man did us well.

7th January.—Monday, nearly overslept, so far as meeting the Fort George was concerned, as she got in about three hours ahead of time. Met the boss, who has had a pretty bad time of it in New York. As far as I can see, nothing but the most artistic lying has got him out of the mess, which appears to be the best way of evading anything in Eastern America. Just sit down and deny that you are alive, and the will bury you for $1,000. Busy at all sorts of things for the rest of the day.

8th January.—Ship's business all day. Handed over my cash, amounting to $15,600, and wired for new cables and anchors to New York.

Got smuggled aboard the dockyard boat by a fellow Scot, and had a trip round to arrange for them to run up two bearings for us. Met another Scot, and he got me dinner in the kitchen of the canteen.

9th January.—After arranging with the chief to catch the nine boat, I went off to the ship at 8:30, and found him still asleep; so we didn't start till twelve. Deuce of a job getting the bearings to the shop. We had taken cycles with us, so we slung them on a piece of wood balanced on our saddles and wheeled them round that way. Lunch consisted of a loaf of bread with butter plastered on it, a hunk of cheese and a tin of apricots; this we ate sitting on the shore. Had a very delightful run home to Hamilton. The island of Somerset is very beautiful, the finest part of Bermuda that I have seen.

10th January.—Busy all day at ship's business. Paid off three of the deck-hands. The blighters expected a bonus for bolting. By the by, I am sleeping at one of the bigger hotels—quite a decent place. Mac came down with the boss. He is a smart lad, and has been showing us how draughts ought to be played. Mac, the boss, Doc, and Hamman are off to the theatre tonight, so I have a little peace to write up some letters.

11th January.—Theatre last night was not a success, for the party came back early. Nothing much doing today. At seven I met the chief engineer, second and Doc, and acted as host on the boss's behalf at dinner in the hotel. After dinner we all (that includes Hamman & Co.) went down to the Palm Gardens. Mac and the second got two partners and danced. They brought some of their friends over, and we all had a dance. It was quite a cheery evening, all told. Doc got very sentimental and was told off severely. Got back to the hotel at 12:30 a.m.

12th January.—Had a long lie, at least until 9:30. Breakfast in my room. Others went for a drive in the afternoon, while I wrote letters and had a sleep. After dinner listened to the hotel orchestra for a little; then got my gear together, as my holiday ashore is over and I return to the fold. Got on board about nine and went straight to sleep.

13th January.—Got up at 6:30, and woke Peters so that we could have breakfast in decent time; no cook at present. The boss and Mac arrived out at 9:15, and demanded eighteen different kinds of paint in as many minutes. Put in a good day painting and chipping. As we expect to sell this ship, we have to keep her looking smart. Expected to have a quiet evening, but the mate brought some of his friends off and put a stop to that. They left about 10:45, when I turned in. Got a touch of rheumatism.

15th January.—Rotten day; very heavy rain. Intended going out to the dockyard by their own boat, but she didn't turn up, so I had to hire a small open motorboat. It was pretty dirty when we got out of shelter, and the boat was half full of water. Coming back the engine stopped half a dozen times, and twice nearly landed us in trouble. The first time we drifted on to the breakwater; the second we just missed a jagged reef. However, we got back safely, to find all hands trying to mend the Downton pump on deck, with slight success so far as I can see. Spent evening peaceably and quietly. Yesterday we nearly had a bad smash with the engine. The chain on which No. 3 piston is hung suddenly broke owing to the vibration. Down it came, and by pure chance the connecting-rod fell over the pin on the shaft. The skirt of the piston got broken a bit, and the vibration of running on three cylinders has jumped the after steering compass off the gimballs and twisted the card, otherwise there was no damage.

16th January.—Spent today chipping— hammer in hand. The boss and Mac have donned overalls and are very busy. Mac is painting the rail round the stern, while the boss, with a chipping-hammer in one hand, a paint-brush in the other, and a scraper behind each ear, keeps about nine jobs going at once and finishes none. Went ashore in the evening and had dinner in the Hamilton Hotel.

Today we got a cook, a Swiss from one of the hotels here—I hope a decent cook at last. Dinner and tea, his only meals so far, have been excellent. Our 12-in. manila hawser has arrived, and is some hawser—4-1/8 in. thick, 120 fathoms long. No fear of breaking away from anchors now, I should say.

17th January.—Busy day with chipping paint and making up store sheet for a problematical voyage of two extra months. There is a party on board—in fact, two. The mate, Doc and second engineer have three ladies out and are treating them to ship's biscuits and tea, plus whisky and port. Judging from the condition of the cabin when I came on board at eleven, the going had been good.

18th January.—Another busy day. Went alongside and took on our manila hawser; it weighs 1-1/2 tons, so had to be handled carefully. Used the new fore-gaff as a derrick. Also took on five tons of coal. When we came to bend the new hawser on the anchor we found it wouldn't go through the shackle. Had intended putting old chain ashore and lying to the hawser in harbour. Result, back to our proper place in the bay to wait for a proper ring. The boss luckily managed to find the very thing in the shape of a real swivel. There's a big job ahead in the engineroom to take off a cylinder and clean the banjo-ring out. Two days' work at least. At last I am having an evening to myself, being at present the only member of our party on board. Have signed on three new fellows this week. Two are soldiers and one is a cabinetmaker, so I don't know how things will pan out this next trip. None of them can take a wheel, but it is impossible to get sailors here for *this* job.

19th January.—Did a good day's work today. The Sabbath won't recover from the smashing we gave it. Started at nine to take a cylinder off. By one the whole thing was adrift, and I fished a heavy piece of wire out of the oil duct in the crank-pin; it was about 6 in. long, so no wonder we ran bearings. This was our Sunday.

20th January.—This morning the mate's brother came off, and, as he had invested in a schooner in Newfoundland, which is held up by the ice, he asked to be allowed to put 200 cases on board us and sail up with it, and sell the lot himself, to gain experience. Much against my wishes, the boss has consented. I don't like it. I feel there is something behind this as he has none too good a reputation ashore, and we are asking him $1 more per case freight than another schooner that's here. I happened to find this out from the skipper of the said schooner. Spent evening on board.

21st January.—Busy all day. In the evening chief engineer and I went ashore to go and see a local theatrical show called *The Eleventh Commandment*. Went into the Regal Prince for a drink. I told the chief I didn't like the idea of this fellow coming with us. He said, "What's that? Neither do I." In the upshot he told me that he had been asked, "Will you be on my side if I come off with a boatload of men and rush the ship the next time you are off the coast?"

So that was it. I was sure there was something, and it will have to be stopped. I wonder if his brother, who is our mate, is in it. Went to the show, a terrible affair.

22nd January.—This has been a good morning. Our friend arrived in a motorboat with his 200 cases at 11:30 a.m. I had already told the boss and Hamman what the chief had told me. The boss, naturally, went off the deep end, and the man got an uncomfortable time of it. An accusation like that, broadcasted, might lead to all sorts of trouble, so, as he had paid for his cargo, we decided to buy it from him and put it on board for ourselves. Fortunately it was good stuff. Gave him what he had paid for it and got rid of him that way. He wasn't at all happy when I had him in the saloon squaring up. The mate is in this also, I'm afraid, for he came with a very glib suggestion that he could put four or five good men on board that would work their passage up for nothing, as they wanted to get smuggled into the U.S.A.—a very pretty scheme. With the mate and his four friends on board to take us in the back, and his brother arriving alongside with some of the pirate fraternity, I fancy we should have been up against it. The boss and the mate came to words over something manufactured by the boss, who told him to pack up. He went, of course. All the same, it's funny business, as he has been a dashed nice chap all along. Didn't go ashore, and turned in about 8:30

25th January.—Signed on a new mate. I fancy he will want watching. Had an evening alone on board.

27th January.—Very busy all day, running here and there seeing that nothing had been forgotten. I expect a good deal will have been, but we shall find that out later. (We didn't.) This is Sunday, so I lay in until nine. Spent a good part of the day doing a painting, or, rather, two paintings, one for a calendar and the other a drawing I did the day the chief and I cycled down from the dockyard. Spent a quiet evening on board with some friends of Cheery's, who paid us a visit. One of them was a very interesting lad—an airman who has been flying in Newfoundland and was employed by the seal-fishers to circle round and find which way the floes are coming down from the north with the young seals, so that they can inter-cept them before they take to the water. His next job, he thinks, is going to be flying with diamonds from the interior of Brazil to the port of shipment. That should be interesting enough.

28th January.—This was my busy day. Got all my stores on board first thing and checked them; then ordered some more, of the luxurious kind, such as tinned salmon, herring, and tripe. Our cables have arrived, so we went alongside the New York steamer, and had them passed down to us in fifteen fathom lengths. It was a splendid pantomime to watch for a bit, with the boss on the steamer, the stevedore, the mate and the captain all shouting orders at once, and everyone tying themselves and the chain into knots. The captain got fed up, so he and I went off to finish some things and get our accounts squared. Two of our disgruntled crew tackled us on the bonus question. When one said he had been consulting a lawyer, the skipper told him to go and see him again. They went along to the ship and interviewed the boss, and got hunted for their pains. Skipper and I had a consultation and decided to get our clearance papers at once. So off we toddled to the Customs House for the articles, and I then had the job of writing up the clearance book. When we got back the boss was on the bridge playing tunes on the engineroom telegraph, and having the time of his life skippering the ship out to a new anchorage. Spent the early part of the evening finishing my checking of accounts. This little jaunt has cost about £2,300 all told (can't buy cables and anchors and have them shipped from New York for nothing), not counting hotel expenses, which can't have been small. Later on we ran into the chief engineer and the second and adjourned to the Palm Gardens. Hamman turned up, very well, thank you. The boss promptly borrowed all the money he had left, so that put the brake on him. Maloney, his right-hand man, has arrived, and is a decent fellow, I think. Our friend the airman also joined us, and we all went off in his motorboat to the ship. Steered a somewhat peculiar course, but got there in the end. He came on board for a little, but went back to sleep in the motorboat, which we passed astern at the end of a painter. Turned in at 1 a.m.

A TYPICAL RUM-RUNNER

BOOK II

CHAPTER I

BACK TO RUM ROW

29th January.—Off on our travels again. Got anchor up at seven, and, after consigning Hamilton to various places, left it astern. We have a peculiar crew this time, in all conscience. Two of the new members have not been to sea before, and one of the others, I think, is a wee bit potty. One had to be paid off sick yesterday, so we are a sailor short. There are only two men who can take a wheel, and these are the Glasgow lads, who are good sorts and stick by the ship. Strong easterly wind when we came outside. Could hardly make headway. The New York boat, with the boss on board, passed us about one hundred yards off, and greetings were duly exchanged. Fair swell running. One of the new cables, 120 fathoms of 8 in. stud link chain, in 15-fathom lengths, is still lying on deck along with two anchors. This bunch immediately started to take charge. Very nice to have 120 fathoms heavy chain and two big anchors walking about the deck, and I thought one of them was going to carry away a steam-pipe. We lashed them as well as possible. New fellows all seasick, but got to work all the same. Wind now E. by S., so we are on our course.

30th January.—Fine bright day. Maloney not at present in love with the sea or this ship. Did 120 miles up to midday, which was not bad. Nothing much doing during the day, but the evening was a 'beezer.' Saw a Jack-o'-lantern for the first time, a most peculiar effect. About midnight a globe of fire, phosphorescent, appeared on the truck of the flagpole and glimmered away for a long time. I believe St. Elmo's Fire is the correct name for it.

31st January.—A dirty night, with heavy thunder and lightning; about 3 a.m. the wind changed into the N.W. It cleared a little about 6:30 a.m., but is not looking quite so nice now. Forenoon very heavy, with rain squalls and wind. At six this morning the fore topmast staysail blew away, tearing loose from the gaskets and making off like a scared bird. So that is an old friend who has stuck by us since Glasgow gone west. Tinned herring for breakfast. During the day the ship rolled very heavily. The anchor cable that is piled on deck has the forepart of the ship absolutely to itself, and charges about in rather a disconcerting fashion, which would spell broken ankles to anyone who tried to interfere with its amusements, while the row it makes on the steel deck is so appalling that no one in the fo'c'sle can sleep. So far the only damage it has done is to tear away the iron ladders to the fo'c'sle head, and, just lately, the windlass steam-pipe and its casing. This is the result of being chased out to sea before there was time to get it shackled together and into the chain locker. It's a mercy one of them is in its proper place. It was easy to lash the two anchors, but short lengths of chain are another story.

1st February.—The new mate has the wind up properly owing to the rolling of the *Cask*; he doesn't know her yet or it would be even further up. He spent a good part of the night running to the captain to say the wind had changed and asking what he was to do? What was really the matter was that the gentleman at the wheel had let the ship go off her course considerably, so that the wind struck her in a different quarter. It evidently didn't occur to the blighter to look at the compass; his nerves had taken charge. Wait till she does some real rolling! Up most of the night, and fell in for a good cup of tea at 4 a.m. Weather today A 1. Fell calm about midday, so immediately after dinner we started to shackle the new anchor cable together and get it into the chain locker. That took three good hours, during which we twice nearly came to losing bits overboard—small matters of fifteen fathoms; however, we didn't. The deck where the anchor cable had been amusing itself is polished like silver. Only did eighty miles in the last twenty-four hours.

2nd February.—Not much doing today. Good breeze. Ship rolling as usual. Thank goodness we have the anchor cable safely out of the way, so that we get a little peace on deck. No excitement took place. Went off to bed early and read Captain Lecky.

3rd February.—Sunday, had two bits of mild excitement. Firstly, when a barrel of salt beef was ordered up on deck, the mate sent pork instead. Two of the fellows below reported the beef was finished. Shock number one. However, I went down, and, after delving amongst a lot of firewood, found the two truant barrels of beef. I was thankful that they had not in some mysterious way been stolen, as it would have left us very short. The next excitement might have been much more serious. Ping Pong and I were having a cup of tea at four bells in the afternoon; when he had finished, off he went to the engineroom, where he was on watch. About half a minute after leaving the messroom I heard him shout, "Fire! fire! Mr. Mac, come." So off I went with a fire extinguiser, and found the fuel valve on No. 1 cylinder had come adrift and the roof and forward bulkhead were dripping blazing oil. Got that out with wet bags plus extinguisher after considerable trouble. No. 3 hatch is just through the bulkhead, so we had the cover off to see if any heat had penetrated the bulkhead, not wanting a whisky fire, thank you. The bulkhead was fairly warm. We are about one hundred miles off the coast, so, as the wind is light, we have taken down sail and are going up under engine only. Making good progress. Am going to turn in early tonight.

CHAPTER II

ANOTHER GALE

4th February.—Cold this morning, but not so cold as I had expected. Nothing much doing in the forenoon; anchored in twenty-six fathoms. Captain waiting for the sun at noon to check his position. Weather fairly thick, and we cannot see far. However, at half-past two we decided to move in a bit. Deuce of a job getting the anchor up. The cable had been dumped down the chain locker anyhow, and the shackles won't fit the gipsy, so we had to pass a messenger to the forward winch and heave every damned one over the top of the gipsy that way. I'm a little bit ahead. At 6:15 a.m. captain woke me and asked if I would mind letting the anchor go. I did so; several of the shackles had to be bashed through the compressor with a Monday hammer. Let out 105 fathoms and left it at that. (Now we go back to the beginning again.) After much messing about of this nature, we managed to get the damned thing up. Went in about six miles. Bos'n was allowed to drop the anchor this time, and let the first shackle run so fast into the compressor that it cracked it. The next job was bending an anchor on to the port cable and getting that overboard. That took about two hours. Got pretty chilly, standing on the fo'c'sle head for all that time. Excellent tea, however. Think we can see Montauk Light about twelve miles off. Inclined to breeze up a bit from the east.

5th February.—I see I wrote that it was inclined to breeze up a bit. The inclination was there, well backed up by the power to do it. In fact, it rose to something over half a gale during last night, and today has been blowing a full gale, with a very ugly sea from the open

Atlantic. About three this afternoon the compressor on the fo'c'sle gave way and the cable started to run out. Fortunately the brake was pretty hard on, and gave time to get it stopped, otherwise we should have lost a new cable. It would have been the boss's own fault for not allowing us time to see if the new shackles fitted.

6th February.—Blew hard nearly all night. In the early morning the wind shifted into the north a bit. Got up anchor about eleven, and started off to the east to look for Montauk Point. Found we had twenty miles to go. Dropped anchor about 4:30 in twenty-six fathoms. There is a very strong tide where we are, though the wind is from the N.W. and we don't face up to it. Saw a fast launch in the distance. Skipper blew his whistle, at which sign of animation on our part, thinking possibly we were the cutter, he turned tail and made for home as fast as he could. Later, about seven, three mysterious boats were reported to have circled us. So I issued out ammunition, etc., and generally we prepared for action. Wind getting stronger. No boats are likely to come near us tonight; getting too rough. We are lying in the trough of the sea left by the easterly gale we had, and are rolling in a deuce of a way. A pot of peas the cook had soaking in view of tomorrow's supper decanted itself over the alleyway and galley. It was like trying to get about on roller skates, standing on those peas. Yarned till twelve with Maloney.

7th February.—The cold last night woke me up several times. There is a little snow this morning, and the ship is rolling damnably— just as badly as she has ever done. On one occasion the bridge was flooded. We are playing the most idiotic game conceivable here just now. If we unload 100 cases a week we are in luck. It is also just approaching the limit of discomfort. I have made a Japanese violin out of a cigar-box. One of the fellows forward has a mandolin, so I have borrowed a spare string of his. The puzzle is going to be what to get for a bow. That I haven't solved yet. The rest are, I expect, hoping I won't manage to solve it either. The time is 1:30 p.m., and we are just going to move again to try to get out of this tide-race. I wish us every success.

8th February.—Very cold, freezing all day, and, I think, all last night also. Spent a busy day making a set of chessmen out of the wood pillars round the back of the settee, the kings and queens from the knobs on the ends of the curtain rods, the knights out of a board off a whisky case. It's a good thing many sets are not required, or I should have half the cabin dismantled to supply the necessary material. The second engineer, Doc and self spent the evening (somewhat alcoholically) in a fierce discussion on biblical history, during which several new points of interest in the Old Testament cropped up which I don't think are generally known. From that the conversation switched on to the 'ideal in woman-hood,' with somewhat mixed results, the ideals of one prominent member of the debating society being so much at variance with his actions that his motions were ruled out of order and the conversation was in danger of becoming acrimonious. That ended the evening's entertainment. Maloney sat and listened and looked the epitome of silent mirth. Anyhow, he has told me that it was better than going to a 'dime' show, whatever that may be.

9th February.—Saturday, and no sign yet of any interest being taken in us by those on shore. Perfect weather, clear and cold; bright sun all day. The lifeboats have about a foot of ice in them which had to be chipped out with axes. Played Cheery four games of chess, and won three. I haven't had time yet to make pawns, so we used instead revolver cartridges, which were excellent substitutes. In the afternoon had a game of deck-skittles with hatch-wedges, an invention of the chief engineer's, which went well.

10th February.—No sign or chance today, I am sorry to say, of any communication with the shore. It's blowing hard from S.W. Wind increased in violence during the night to a full gale, with a very big sea. Our old cables would no more have stood this strain than butter would have. Rolling as badly as she has ever done. In fact, she had been rolling the water across her bridge, which she has only done once before. That was when we lost the gaff and foresail in the Gulf Stream coming up the first time. Very cold still.

11th February.—A devil of a night. Wind shifted into the north, and, as usual, left us in the trough of a deuce of a sea. Early in the morning skipper thought he would drop the second anchor. Found the manila hawser had swollen in the hawse pipe so much that the chain was jammed and anchor wouldn't go down. Fo'c'sle head a mass of ice. Tried to bash the anchor down with a fore-hammer, but couldn't keep my feet on the ice with her rolling, so that had to be left to another time. Got a roaring fire going down aft, and turned in fairly early.

Got two cases tinned meat up from the afterhold. Got steam up to get anchor freed from the hawser, and found all the pipes were frozen. Took about two hours to unfreeze. Snowing heavily, wind E.N.E. and very cold. No chance of boats today. Nothing much doing otherwise. Practised my concertina for a bit, and finished the chessmen.

CHAPTER III

SELLING THE STUFF

13th February.—Today has brought one of the surprises of this game. We spent the morning clearing snow from the deck, and at ten a three-masted schooner came and hove to near us. Dropped a boat, rowed over, and came on board. They were a couple of hard cases, after water and coal. We gave them two bags of coal and two barrels of water. They have lost their anchors, and have to spend the time cruising about with only a kedge and fifty fathoms chain left. At three a small two-master hove to under our stern and came with the same request; we gave no coal but a little water. Very cold, but clear and bright. Took two photographs of the crew. Then came the surprise. We were giving the second schooner his water when a launch was spotted coming alongside. He wanted as much as we could give him, and took 500 cases. Just as we had finished that lot, another boat arrived—this time a small sailing-boat. He went off with 430 of the best; 930 cases in three hours' work. There aren't going to be many cash transactions here, I can see, for which I'm not sorry. No mail for me yet. I wonder what has happened to my letters: I have had none since 18th December, and this is now 13th of February. There must be a good pile of them somewhere. A certain amount of alcohol was consumed on board, and captain had to get on the rampage. Cook got a snowball on the ear through a port in the galley. As he is somewhat excitable, he raised hell to some tune and played several kinds of bands, principally jazz. He has a wee white and black fox terrier on board, which sleeps in his room. It's quite a nice wee doggie, but gets vicious when we are rolling much and he is seasick. The other day the wash ports were lashed open, and as nearly as anything he went through. We start the old watches tonight. I take with the mates, and the Doc with the engineers. My first spell is from four to eight tomorrow morning. We have had some more visitors. A launch, looking for the first schooner to which we gave coal, came to us, and, as it has breezed up a good deal and they are frightened to go the eighteen miles to the shore, they are lodged in the fo'c'sle while their boat rides aft to a painter. If it blows much harder they will lose her.

14th February.—Our visitors were in luck. The breeze that looked very like freshening changed its mind and died down about 2:30 a.m. Went on watch at four. Very cold. At 6:30 a.m. the wind looked like getting worse, so I woke our two Greeks and started to get them off. Their boat was nearly frozen up, with icicles festooned all over it. Had to cut the ropes (painter), as the knots were too frozen to untie. Their engine wouldn't start, most of their petrol having run out of the tank through a broken joint which we repaired for them. Maloney has had enough, and decided to go ashore, so off he went with them. I would rather stay where I am this morning, as it looks like a nor'-wester. When they had got about five miles off, they started to come back. However, the cutter *Manhattan* came over from the west to interview us, and they made a bolt for it. Nothing much doing the rest of the day, except getting up the anchor and shackling on the 12-inch manila. Very cold on deck today; snowing most of the time.

15th February.—Slept very badly last night. At 1:30 the ship started to roll like the deuce. This lasted for about two hours. We got the hawser over the side and are now waiting for a wind sufficiently strong to draw the cable taut. Our manila and the chain won't both go through the hawse pipe, so the manila is made fast round the foremast and passes over the fo'c'sle head. Its job is to take the first jerk when sou'-easters blow up and big seas come in from the Atlantic. It should save another cable parting.

16th February.—About noon a three-masted schooner passed within fifty yards of our stern and I got a couple of photographs, which should be good. Played chess in the evening with the second engineer, and won. Did some wee drawings, and painted them with gum to prevent the pencil rubbing off. Beautiful evening, but no sign of business. Expected Maloney back tonight.

17th February.—Sunday, a perfect day, though cold. Last night it snowed a little and froze a lot; result, plenty of ice about the deck this morning. Very cold out of the sun. Many degrees of frost, I should say. Did a painting in the afternoon of a snow scene. Very fine! No sign of business again today. It is time we heard something more from the shore. Played chess again in the evening. Am on watch twelve till four tomorrow, so turned in at ten to have a couple of hours' sleep. That is what I did last night, I mean. The mate forgot to call me, and let me sleep on till two. Result, no one on watch for two hours.

18th February.—Another beautiful day, and warm, for a wonder. Got out my 'goose' and had some practice, also wrote out three tunes. That filled a good part of the morning. About three a cry of "Boat in sight." Much excitement. It was the same boat as came on the 13th, and he took 501 cases. He also brought us fresh meat, vegetables and six old hens, which don't look as though they had been properly brought up. After tea, in the middle of a game of chess with the Doc, another cry of "Boat," but he only took 75 cases. At midnight I found no one on watch. Someone will need to be talked to in the morning seriously. I know who it is, but we'll mention no names at present. Went on deck in my stocking soles, and it wasn't too warm.

19th February.—I heard rather an amusing tale this morning. When the second boat came alongside yesterday, the Doc and I were playing chess. He is a bit of a pedant, and gets many a leg-pull. He acts as tally clerk, as he can be trusted not to slip two or three extra cases over, for which little service he tells me he is often offered $10 for himself. On this occasion he went on deck without a hat or coat, and sent the mess-boy down to his room for them. The chief and second engineers happened to be there, and as the Doc has all his wordly goods on board, they sent him back with a dinner-jacket, pot-hat and walking-stick. Quite a good dress in which to discharge cargo on a frosty night. When the mess-boy produced this assortment, he was greeted with, "Well, what the hell disease have you got now?" However, he saw the joke and the possibility of tallying the cargo on his white shirt-front. There was no word of Maloney yesterday. Hamman has sent a note to him here, so evidently he has not yet got in touch with the people in New York. I hope he is all right.

20th February.—Last night it started to breeze hard from the S.E. When I came on watch at 4 a.m. it was blowing a full gale, and that went on all day, with a very nasty sea running. With the starboard compressor gone, the whole weight of the ship is on the windlass, and it looks rather like leaving the deck. At two, Cap thought he would drop the port anchor, but the second shackle jammed. I found them trying to hammer it through. There was steam in the donkey-boiler, and evidently one of our soldier-sailors had been trying his hand at driving the windlass by letting the chain slack, and then giving her full steam in reverse, in the hope the jerk would release the shackle; with the result that the starboard connecting-rod, the casting holding a main bearing, and also an eccentric strap, are broken. That's that. Can't use the blinking thing now, as these repairs are beyond us. I expect it will be a sweet job getting the anchor up with the hand-gear when we have to quit. Before it was found that the windlass was out of action, this drastic method had borne fruit, and away went the port chain a-roaring. Whoever was in charge of the brake let her run too fast, and bang!—the third shackle had caught where the chain pipe enters the locker. It twisted the pipe and an angle beam, and then the shackle burst open. So away went another anchor, and with it forty-five fathoms of our chain. Don't know quite why, but expect this shackle must have been bent on the wrong way in the hullabaloo in Hamilton. Turned in at eight, but it was rolling too much for sleep.

21st February.—A very uncomfortable day. My watch is from eight to twelve. At the time of writing the wind is rising rapidly again, and we look like getting another gale from the west for a change. Glass is rising, though.

We are all getting very bad-tempered, I find, and too easily irritated. I'm afraid this life is beginning to get on my nerves a bit. Today I wanted to get Cap to unshackle the starboard chain from the locker and make it fast round the foremast, so that if the windlass goes it will need to take the whole fore part of the ship with it, which can't happen. But so far he hasn't done it.

22nd February.—Blowing pretty strongly from the west all day. No boats visited us. The fresh meat the first boat brought out is now finished and we are back to salt horse again. Bos'n down with his kidneys—lumbago, he says; 'rumbago,' I think, is nearer the mark. Had a row with the mate today, and told him to take his something hands out of his pockets and do some work or I would set about him. He looked rather annoyed, but did as he was told. There is a steamer somewhere round, I have been told, that is supposed to be smuggling cocaine and Chinese. I fancy she was the one that came and had a look at us this morning.

23rd February.—Very sleepy this morning, and didn't get up till 8:30. Now that Maloney has gone ashore I have the benefit of his quilt, and am not looking forward to him coming back and claiming it. Got my way about the anchor chain round the mast today. Have shackled up other anchor on to the port cable. Took fifteen fathoms off the other, so that one has five shackles and the other has eight. Still cold. Wind shifting into the N.E. I am on watch from twelve to four, and expect it will be chilly, as the stove in the chartroom won't light properly. Have been practising my chanter a bit, also the concertina. Discovered some new combinations on the concertina this evening. Quite well pleased with myself.

24th February.—A perfect day; just cold enough to give you an appetite, and hardly a ripple on the water. About three in the afternoon along comes a boat with Maloney on board. He brought an assortment of things out to us. As far as I am concerned, I was most interested in a pair of felt-lined snow boots. So no more cold feet on deck, I hope. He generously relieved us of 695 cases, which was by no means too bad. He intended bringing out a side of beef, but unfortunately, the day being Sunday, the butcher's shop was closed. However, I daresay he will bring some next trip. Sent our broken windlass parts ashore to be repaired. It appears there is a good deal of ice ashore, and I'm not surprised, for the temperature out here has not been exactly tropical. Some of the boats must have about six inches of ice to break through to get out to us. Doc and skipper had a set to for a bit, but it soon blew over. Broached cargo today to the extent of one bottle, sample size, of Chartreuse. The boss wanted one case of samples ashore. I didn't know which was the sample size, so had to open cases to find out. Found out and tried one, which was very good. Wish I had taken another.

25th February.—Another fine day; in fact, the kind on which it is difficult to believe this is the American coast in winter, after all the stories one has heard about it. We shall probably pay for it later on. Spent nearly all day writing up statistics for the boss, and hope he will enjoy digesting them. Had some customers this afternoon, but there was not much doing with them. One fellow says the boss told him he could buy at twenty. I wouldn't be surprised if he did say so, but this boss here (ME) said, "Nothing doing." I think I shall be able to unload the gin on to another fellow at eighteen. I have offered the lot to him at that figure, so we shall see. Gin can be easily made ashore, so they won't pay much out here for it.

26th February.—Fine weather still with us. Expected friend Maloney back today, but he didn't put in an appearance. Others did, though, and we had a fairly good day, getting rid of 784, which is not too bad. We had two new customers, including one fellow who should prove quite a good hauler, his first load from us being 170 He was quite a late arrival, in fact, blew in about 8:30 and didn't get away until after midnight. It was dead calm, so he would have a good run in. I am getting quite a collection of dollar bills—about twenty-two thousand at present. I should like to go ashore when I have forty thousand and get rid of it! So much hard cash is a temptation out here. Wrote today to my pal, who is playing at the Times Square Theatre. If I get ashore I must run into New York and give him a surprise. Our lifeboats had again about a foot of ice in them this morning, so part of the day was spent in digging it out.

27th February.—Wind gradually getting into the N.W., and in consequence becoming colder. Spliced up some fishing-line and made fast the lamp in the cabin, as it is threatening to break loose from the roof owing to the rolling. This morning the rudder of a ship floated past us; thirteen feet was marked on it, so she must be a fair-sized vessel, and someone will be spending an uncomfortable time of it, I am afraid. Held an audit on myself this afternoon and found myself correct. So far I have only managed to miscount $20 (one note) out of $84,460, so that's not bad. Unfortunately, it is on the wrong side. No letters yet from home; I wonder if they are being held up on purpose. When I came off watch just after midnight I found the cabin in the hell of a mess. The coal-bunker was upset, coal was all over the place, and the chairs were rolling about the floor. The stove had emptied itself of red-hot coal, which was mingled with the other in a mad fandango. It is a good thing the floor is made of a fireproof composition.

28th February.—A fine day as far as clearness is concerned, but cold—at least the wind is nippy, and plenty of frost is still about. We have had it down as far as 20 degrees of frost, which is quite cold enough. No boats today; sea too choppy. Nothing much doing. Re- stowed some of the cases in two of the holds. That took up a good part of the day.

1st March.—Another Saturday! I wonder how many more I shall see before we empty the damned ship. Got rid of some stuff today, thank goodness. Maloney arrived out at 2:45 and brought fresh meat, milk, sugar, cigarettes with him, so that is always something. What he took away with him was even more important, namely, 566 cases of the best—at least, 100 of the worst we have, and 466 others. Not the worst from the point of view of quality, because all our stuff is good, but from the point of view of what they call cutting. A great deal of the whisky sold out here reaches the consumer as it leaves us, that is, if it is going to one of the good clubs, first-class hotels or any of the wealthier homes or good restaurants; all of them have their own private bootlegger or firm of bootleggers, who deliver the proper goods. But, on the other hand, a great quantity when it gets ashore is blended with crude alcohol and heaven knows what else—one bottle of, say, 'Old Smuggler' making four bottles of what the consumer thinks is 'Old Smuggler.' The brand I call the worst, for some reason or another, won't mix as well—or cut as well, to use the shore term. Maloney brought a sheaf of papers out, and the cabin tonight looks like the back shop of a bill-posting establishment. The boss says in a note I got that he is sending out a radio set. I suppose that is a kind of bribe to us to stay out here indefinitely. Well, we will see. He tells me in his note that the ship will be in danger if I leave it. I don't know what he means by that exactly. What is quite certain is, if it were left to the present deck officers there would be very little unbroken on board in a fortnight. Have had a rotten headache for about four days now. Have been T.T. for the last three weeks, but can't say I feel any better for it.

CHAPTER IV

A REAL SPORTSMAN

2nd March.—Sunday, nothing doing today. Have started a competition with the bos'n as to who can do the smallest splice. I started with a heavy fishing-line, while he replied with a somewhat lighter one. I did a lighter, and so did he. I'll need to start on linen thread to beat him now. That nonsense filled part of the day, a sleep filled some more.

3rd March.—Another fine day. March is coming in like a lamb this year. Quite warm on deck and an oil calm. Have been studying the question of latitude and longitude for the last four months on and off, and my placing of the ship at present differs by only a quarter of a mile from the captain's. If it should by some strange freak be necessary I would chance taking her home, as only myself and skipper can use a sextant or read a chart. Met a real sportsman today. He came out alone in a small motorboat about eighteen feet long with a single cylinder engine. Doing that here is as though a man were to set out from the coast of Cornwall and make eighteen miles out into the Channel at a time of the year when dirty weather arrives with little or no warning. He was a west of Ireland man, judging by his accent. He has a cork leg, but managed to come over the side all right. He took 20 cases, and I gave him $5 discount for coming out this distance by himself. He promises to come back. Have started to splice a silk thread (a suture), so we'll see if the bos'n beats that. Maloney arrived out in his fishing boat and wandered off with 573 cases; that's what we want to see. A perfect night. Gave the chief engineer a brief but succulent account of our universe and the possibilities of others outside of it. Retired to rest early, as I am on the morning watch. *i.e.*, 4 a.m. till 8 a.m.

4th March.—Another glorious day. Hardly a breath of wind. Our sportsman of yesterday was back again—more power to him!—and took 31 cases this time. I gave him one for himself at $20 instead of $23. Completed my splice with the aid of a magnifying glass and handed it over to Mr. Bos'n. Another lonely gentleman came today and took 19, so he also got a small discount, fifty cents this time. Weather not looking so well in the evening, cloudy, and inclined to breeze up, I think, from the S. I am on watch from eight till midnight.

5th March.—It didn't breeze up after all. Fine day for unloading. Expected Maloney out, but no sign of him. I am afraid, as far as rapidity of discharge is concerned, Hamman is going to prove a broken reed. The trouble is that he has to take the stuff all the way up Long Island Sound, nearly seventy miles. Not quite so warm as yesterday, yet quite a mild spring day. Practised at the concertina, but it will be some time yet before I shall be able to make a real job of it. Have been holding a series of lectures on the art of landscape drawing, with the second engineer as the class.

6th March.—Nearly a week of March gone, and still calm. There must be a gale brewing somewhere. A small colony of birds have taken up their abode with us. One arrived this morning, very tired, and five others have come at intervals of about an hour. They are not unlike sparrows, but brighter in plumage, and are becoming quite friendly. They may be the advance guard of the migratory birds returning to the northern part of America. If so, that is a sign that winter here is coming to an end. Crew are busy trying to see if they can make the bridge deck leak, and, judging from the second engineer's remarks, are being remarkably successful. His room is under the starboard side of the bridge. Retired to bed early, as I am on watch from twelve until four tomorrow.

7th March.—The cutter was round about 2 a.m. this morning, having a look at her charges with her searchlight. Last night I was wakened by our bell ringing. Fog had come down and a big steamer was blowing in the vicinity. Don't want anyone running into us during the night, thank you. Wrote some letters while on watch. The *Star* has arrived back, damn her! That means another 25,000 cases, all told, in this neighbourhood. I suppose round here there must be about 90,000 cases to be disposed of, and the Lord knows when that will be absorbed, as I daresay more ships are on the way out now that the fine weather is setting in.

8th March.—I see I wrote 'now that the fine weather is setting in.' This morning it would require a man with seven league boots on, walking for about a fortnight, to find it. It's blowing half a gale from W.N.W. At 2.30 a.m. there was a sharp fall of snow, with the temperature back to somewhere round freezing-point. We have spent the day mostly in our bunks, as it is quite impossible to stand or sit on a chair, The saloon is a sight—chairs, red-hot coal, coal-bucket plus contents, shoes and other articles chasing each other all over the floor. Wired up the stove with wire off whisky cases to keep the contents at home. Spent the afternoon sleeping. This continual rolling hurts one's stomach. Even the bos'n, who has been on sailing ships all his life, said today, "I wish the bloody ship would roll right over and finish it;" and, upon my soul, I sometimes feel the same way. I heard rather an amusing story today. One member of the crew is a Newfoundlander and kind of 'saft in the heid.' One day, on the way up here, the captain sent him aft to see what was on the 'log.' He carefully pulled the twenty-five fathoms of line right in, hoisted the vane inboard, came back to the bridge and reported "Seaweed, sir!" Collapse of captain and hurried retirement of Newfoundlander to the comparative safety of the fo'c'sle. There has been a big blow somewhere to the south of us; result, a rotten cross sea caused by the swell coming up from that quarter. The tide makes us lie broadside to it.

9th March.—On watch this morning 4 a.m. to 8 a.m. Glass rising, but there's no sign of the rolling getting any better. Weather is trying to improve, all the same. Spent part of my watch reading up the South Atlantic Directory, which I found quite interesting. Everybody is in a very bad temper this morning; it would be easy to get up a fine scrap.

10th March.—No improvement in the weather. It's still blowing from the N., fairly hard, and there's no chance of any boats arriving. Spent the day in the engineroom receiving a lesson in splicing wire rope and making slings and straps, with painful results for my fingers. Went on watch at eight. There's every appearance of a nasty blow coming from the N.E., and the glass falling rapidly. As a matter of fact, I never saw a glass drop as ours did between 11:30 and 11:45 p.m., when it came down nearly half an inch. By 11:45 it was blowing a fresh gale. Came off at twelve and turned in. We were shipping some big dollops, and the spray was coming well over the chart-house.

CHAPTER V

WE DRAG OUR ANCHOR

11th March.—Thought so. When I woke at 5:30 this morning she was dipping her nose well into it, the wind was fairly howling, and a tremendous sea was running. She is now practically standing on her tail and her head alternately. The only possible plan is to get well wedged into a bunk and stay there, which I have done. Glass still falling slowly. At three this afternoon it was a good deal lower than at any time during the whole trip. The fo'c'sle crowd can't have their meals there, as nothing can be carried forward; it's too dangerous with a young mountain of water coming right over the fo'c'sle head every few minutes and breaking at the foot of the foremast. I hope the cable holds; so far it has done marvels. Spent most of the day sleeping and reading, with short intervals for meals. Two or three extra big waves about three in the afternoon came over the fo'c'sle, and the wind brought solid water right over the charthouse and landed it on the poop. They were good efforts, and the old *Cask* staggered like anything when they hit her. A few more of these and there would be damage to no mean extent. Had a yarn with the second engineer till about ten, and then turned in.

12th March.—Woke at three this morning and got up to have a look round. Glass at 28.1—the limit—and absolutely blowing smoke. Had a look at it, and came back to bunk again without undue loss of time. At 7 a.m. the glass was rising and wind was inclined to go into the N. Hope it does, for that will mean a less sea, a good deal less in fact. Spent another day confined to bunk, so to speak.

13th March.—On watch from 12 till 4 a.m. No sign of Montauk Light. It looks to me as though we had dragged a bit. At five last evening one of the big Cunarders passed fairly close to us; I remember thinking at the time she must be a bit out of her course, as that is the first of the big ships we have seen since coming back to the coast. Before turning in, I got Morrison to heave the lead, and found thirty- eight fathoms, so we have dragged. Can't do anything. Told the skipper. Blowing hard all watch. Turned in at 4:30 a.m., and was awakened by sounds of heaving the lead again. Found no bottom. As the lead line is forty fathoms, we've dragged a queer bit. At midday the old man got the sun, and found we had managed to drag our anchor a matter of fifty miles during that blow. It is very doubtful if we shall manage to get it back. Here we are, seventy-five miles off land, with an anchor down that we can't lift with half the windlass on shore being repaired. If we drag any more we shall soon get over the hundred-fathom line, and then it will be quite impossible to get it back owing to the weight of cable hanging down. It looks very much as if we should have to slip the cable, which will leave us with a seventy-five fathoms chain and one anchor—just as bad as before It will be a sin to throw away 120 fathoms of new cable, plus the anchor. It looks very like breezing up again tonight, so goodness knows where we shall drag to by the morning. I spent a good part of the day re-studying Morse, and last night during my watch I managed to master the International Flag Alphabet. It won't be of any use, but it was interesting and something to do.

14th March.—Everyone full of vigour this morning, some more so than others. I am not quite sure what happened yet, but, anyhow, there was a row of sorts when Mr. Mate went forward at six and apparently tried to get the men to turn to. I don't see how the mate can expect to get much respect from these fellows when he sneaks into the fo'c'sle and plays cards with them for cigarettes. I asked the Old Man what he thought about it this morning, and I fancy he has, or will, put an end to such amusements. Rigged up the hand-gear on the windlass and attempted to get some chain in before using the main engine. Hopeless. Got main engine going at 1:15 p.m., and tried again with part of the weight of the ship off. No use. Will have another shot at it when we get a proper gun tackle rigged to the foremast and use No. 1 winch. Very cold today. Freezing again and glass going down a little—about four-tenths in four hours. Looks like snow. Am on watch tomorrow morning from 4 a.m. to 8 a.m., so I am going to turn in early and get a reasonable sleep. The chocolate I bought in Hamilton, which I nibble a bit of every night instead of drinking whisky, is nearly finished now, so it looks like having to drink whisky. Most things on board will soon be finished, anyhow. I am afraid we shall have to make a trip to Halifax before we are very much older.

15th March.—Blowing hard all day, with big seas. Hopeless to try to get the anchor in. Glass refuses to rise more than about one twenty-fifth at a time. Then, as if regretting its temerity, it promptly drops back to the beginning again. Nothing much doing all day; saw a small schooner beating up to the N.W. in the afternoon and making very heavy weather of it. Spent part of the day rigging up a suitable tackle for lifting the anchor as soon as the weather moderates. We are now in ninety fathoms, so I'm afraid it won't do. The manila has parted, so that our springer is no longer easing the strain on the chain.

16th March.—Blowing harder than ever, and the glass inclined to drop. At 11:30 this forenoon we gave some wild bucks, and, snap!— away went the cable. So there's our hold on America gone again. We got into the trough of the sea at once and did a queer amount of rolling. Got up the spanker, but that didn't keep her head to it. Discussed with the captain what we should do, and decided to make for Halifax. Gave word to start up the main engine as soon as possible. A big oil tanker thought we were salvage, and came and stood by for about two hours. Hoisted inner jib and took spanker down, but she wouldn't wear round. I took the wheel, and at one time we all thought she was going over. My feet were swung off the deck while holding the wheel; however, she righted, and on the engine starting she came around. Got up foresail and mainsail, and at present—4 p.m.—we are doing about '10 knots before a very fresh gale. Halifax is 630 miles off, so we have at least six days' journey ahead of us. Glass still falling, wind freshening, and a dirty sea running. At 9:30 the engine stopped. Chief reported he thinks rose box in No. 2 tank choked and unable to pump to the supply tank. So the engine is off for the night. I wonder what else is going to happen. A very uncomfortable night, rolling wildly.

17th March.—Worked a good part of the day at unshipping the semi-rotary pump in the engineroom, and replacing it with the galley pump. After priming that, we got oil to come up. We shall save a tug-boat's expense, anyhow. Still a strong gale from the N.W., with a dirty high sea. We are making quite good sailing under foresail and mainsail, about 6-1/2 knots. We can't put any more up, or she won't steer. Feeling very sleepy and tired tonight for some reason or other. Nothing much doing except discomfort.

18th March.—Trouble started early this morning. At 5:30 a.m. we were wakened by the ship broaching to. The second mate came down and reported the steering gear out of action, so I had to get up and examine that. Found the chain had fallen out of its place on the quadrant. The *Cask* had immediately taken the opportunity to get into the trough of the sea and roll like hell, which didn't make work at the quadrant any easier. Woke chief up, and he and I tackled the job. Tried to put the after emergency gear in, but, as luck would have it, just as we were slipping a heavy pin into place, a big wave hit the rudder, one arm of the emergency gear came forward with a bang and sheared the pin, nearly breaking the chief's elbow. At ten the chain fell off again. More work this time; cut out four links with a bow saw, slackened back all the rigging screws, and put on two sail shackles. In the afternoon foresail leech ripped off and sail split near the throat, so had that down and put on the new one we had made in Bermuda. Wind and sea have at last fallen a bit, thank goodness. Eleven days' gale gets monotonous, particularly when every day something fresh breaks. Had a confab, with Cap, and decided we had better make Bermudas again as we had been blown so far south.

19th March.—Extraordinary! Nothing has broken today that matters much; only the foresail took it into its head to split about three in the afternoon. Both mates watched it go and didn't think of doing anything. I suppose they were waiting for darkness, so as to make it easier! However, we got it down before night fell. Nothing else happened, and it is very much warmer.

20th March.—Cigarettes practically finished. I have just enough to last me into Bermuda, provided we get in there tomorrow, as we should do. At 9:30 p.m. a light was sighted, and reported as the light on St. David's Head. On approaching, it proved to be the masthead light of a large steamer, evidently lying off until daylight. Sighted the proper light at 10:15 p.m., about twenty miles off, bearing S.W.1/2 S. Inclined to rain Rumpus this morning between captain and crew. He wanted them to turn out and scrape decks at 6 a.m., which they refused to do. I'm not sorry, for if they had it would have wakened everyone aft at that ungodly hour, and I've a lot of arrears of sleep to make up. Learned how to put a grummet in a leech rope. Checked all my money. I have $65,845 to hand into the bank tomorrow.

RESULT OF ROLLING

U.S. CUTTER *MANHATTAN*

CHAPTER VI

BACK TO BERMUDA

21st March.—Pilot came aboard about 5:45 and we started into the channel. They have had a pretty severe blow here also, and the place is full of shipping in for shelter. A Cunarder, a C.P.R., a Hall boat and many others. Got the anchor down at 9:30. We are too near a small schooner, I think. Got cleaned up and went ashore at twelve to pay in the money, enter the ship and put through the usual formalities. Have heard plenty of tales of disaster since I arrived. Four large ships have foundered. The Halifax mailboat arrived down with all her boats stove in, the starboard rail chewed into knots, her portholes smashed, etc. The Furness Bermuda Line boats have been taking four days to do a two days' trip. In fact, the blow has been worse than we supposed, and we have been lucky to weather it. There is the crew of an Italian steamer that foundered about three hundred miles S.E. of here awaiting repatriation. I have a room in the Royal Hotel with a bath room attached, and intend to live in a modified kind of clover for the next day or two at least. Am writing this up in my room after having several with the second engineer and the Doc, and am feeling a little more contented than before. Went on board about three for a little.

22nd March.—Wind rising a little, so in our usual way we started to drag, and came down alongside the white schooner, who very wisely bolted and anchored again about 200 yards astern of us.

23rd March.—Started the day with a splendid hot bath—an excellent idea. I had just got out, when the telephone rang and

Cheery came up to say the ship had dragged again and was nearly aground. It was blowing far too hard to get out to her, so he and the Doc had slept ashore. Went down to see, and found she had gone about 200 yards. It was blowing smoke, and the harbour was impossible for a small boat. Captain and mate are having the father and mother of a row. Captain has told him that if he doesn't get on board he will have him arrested. Had my hair cut. Entered our protest. Captain got off to the ship about 3:30, and came back in a deuce of a rage. I think he made a bit of an ass of himself on board. Anyhow, the chief engineer let fly at him, and he has forbidden anyone to come on shore. They are sore at that, as they had worked like hatters and got the ship fast to the Ocean Transport tenders' buoy. Morrison spent last night in jail. Fined £1 this morning, which I went and paid. If he does it again they'll give him ten days' hard. He says the jail here isn't as comfortable as the one at home. Spent the evening having a dance, and quite enjoyed myself. I think it is the first care-free evening I have had since leaving England.

23rd March.—Sunday, a better day, though there is still a fresh breeze blowing. I was in my bath at 10 a.m., when the captain came up to say there was a cable from New York. Nothing definite in it, however. Went out to the ship at 11:30, and found a considerable amount of hilarity on board, centred in the bos'n. Cook is also well lit up. Didn't stay very long, but came ashore for lunch. Had a walk in the afternoon and tea in the new Bermudiana, a fine hotel inside. Came back and had dinner, then went back to the Bermudiana and heard a very decent concert—real music, not claptrap.

24th March.—Got up at 7:30, and wandered down to the office to see if there were any cables. Very busy on the ship most of the day. After a lot of trouble we got our anchor up, using a messenger from No. 1 winch, and then left our friend the buoy. We are now back in our old spot, and I hope we stay there this time. Got a bow for my Jap fiddle. It has quite a good tone. Spent the evening after dinner making up my accounts and writing letters. There is a jazz band in full working order in the dancing court just outside my window, which is rather distracting.

25th March.—Wire from the boss today. 'Anchor chains ordered, bringing them myself. Get ship painted. Have oil and stores on board and ship ready sail on my arrival.' Well, we shall see. It depends when he arrives.

Went over to the dockyard this morning to try to get a new compressor cast. Left at nine. There is a new broom over there who is 'new brooming' to some tune. I must produce a certificate that I cannot obtain what I want anywhere else before they will give it me. Lunched off a hunk of bread, some cheese and a small tin of Strasburg paste in a wee pub, and listened to some splendid vituperation between two members of the dockyard labouring department. Came back on the naval duty pinnace on which I had no business to be. Another cable from New York. 'Anchor, etc., being shipped on the 2nd. Get fifteen tons fuel oil.' So that's that.

Drove into St. George's this afternoon to try to get the compressor cast, but it was no use; the people there can't do the work. However, I have a letter to that effect, so perhaps the dockyard will condescend to do it.

26th March.—An extraordinary day. Went down to the landing-place with the idea of going on board, and found half a gale blowing. It was raining hard as well, with a big sea in the bay. The *Cask* was off on its travels again; she managed to drag about 150 yards, but stopped this time on a mooring chain. It's very bad holding ground in the bay here. Torrential rain, accompanied by a heavy thunderstorm. In one gust of wind I saw the roof of a shed lifted and blown away like a kite. Got some of the work at the engine shop finished. Have a fine healthy dose of mosquito bites. I can hardly use my right hand owing to three bites on the wrist; also a darned spider or something has bitten me above the left eye and I can't see out of it.

27th March.—Better day today. Got some work done, and all my stores made up and ordered. Arranged to go over to the dockyard tomorrow with the casting. By the by, I had a treat last night. Found the lounge empty about eight, so had a shot at the piano; it's not much of an instrument, but it was fine to get playing again. My fingers are awful; I can hardly do anything with them now. Spent most of the day on board. The chief and second are coming in tonight to get tight at my expense. There is a variation in the racket outside this evening. Instead of two jazz bands, there is one military band playing 'The Pilgrims' Chorus' and one jazz band playing God knows what. The result is appalling. Skipper has been making himself unpopular on board again, and everyone is fit to cut his throat. I have heard tonight of a captain I can get, with a certificate, if the necessity should arise. He is a temporary barman at present.

28th March.—Started off at 9:30 for the dockyard in a small motorboat with the castings and the cylinder head. Got there with only three stoppages, but had to combat the usual red tape in a battle which lasted for about 1-1/2 hours, and left honours easy, in that I have got them to do the work and they have got me to come back and fill up numerous forms on Monday. Coming back, there was a strong west wind, and, crossing the entrance to the bay, engine gave up again and we started off to try to get in by drifting. Rescued by the Coral Reef boat.

29th March.—Got up at nine and sat about till it was time to go and have dinner with the captain and family. The old chap did us very well. Stayed there until 3:30, then took the ferry over to Belmont to see a friend who is living there. Took the wrong road, and finally reached the hotel via several people's gardens and over their walls. Left at eight and came over to the Bermudiana. Indulged in a porterhouse steak and listened to the Sunday concert. Came back to my *houff* at ten and turned in.

31st March.—Dockyard again. After filling up and signing the necessary forms I found I hadn't sufficient money to pay, so that means another visit tomorrow. Got back at 1:30 and found the oil still on the quay; it should have been taken off at ten. Got that done. Found a broken pulley bracket for the steering chain, so made a drawing of it and put the matter into the engineer's hands.

1st April.—Went out to the dockyard and got my debts paid. They have managed to discover that the last job cost £8 3s. 9d. more, so got that account fixed. Sat on the shore for a bit to put in time waiting for the duty picket boat. Dissected a prickly pear and got one of the prickles into my hand, by way of fee, so to speak. Sent most of the stores out in the afternoon. Am putting plenty on board this time. I expect the boss will kick up his heels, but I'm not going to live on salt horse again all the time. Had quite an interesting evening expounding the difference between Scots and English law to two elderly Americans who pretended they were interested. Also gave them a vivid account of how whisky is distilled, culled principally from my imagination. Hope they don't meet a distiller before we leave.

2nd April.—Busy day today. The Ocean Transport people have intimated that we have punctured their blessed buoy and that the thing is sinking; it certainly looks as though it had gone down a bit. It will soon be a case of the tender holding the buoy up instead of the other way round. That meant a new protest and a special report (i.e., abstract from the log, which was written up afterwards very carefully). Then I had to get stores on board and check them. Had a long chat with the captain barman in the evening, and also had an excellent Welsh rarebit.

3rd April.—Fairly busy again today with odds and ends, such as coal and water. After dinner I got into conversation with two American girls, who asked if there was a piano they could play. One of them played dashed well. I played for a bit, and was surprised to find every blessed visitor in the hotel sitting in the lounge listening. The piano is behind a screen, and you can't see what is going on in the lounge or I wouldn't have done it. Walked up to the Bermudiana to listen to a military band, but found a lantern lecture going on with 'Jungle Life in Malay' as the subject. Very interesting; the slides were excellent.

4th April.—Was in the middle of breakfast when the waiter said the New York boat was docking. Bolted down without finishing my breakfast, but found no signs of her. Cursed the waiter. Skipper had got a pass for the quay. The boss arrived, and the balloon did not go so high as I had thought it might. I think he realises that the last blow we had was a bad one. There was a bit of a racket, all the same. Buzzed about and had a row with our storeman for trying to palm off a barrel of pork on us that the brine had run out of.

5th April.—Devil of a row today over the bonus question. I'm sick of this. The boss goes off the deep end and leaves me to hold the baby. The mate, who is a useless devil, the second mate and two deck-hands all refused to sign off unless they got the bonus. There was a scene in the shipping office, and another on board, when the boss refused to pay any. However, after a good deal of shenanigan, I got him to agree to pay some, as we would never get another hand here if something extra wasn't given.

6th April.—Beautiful day. Bought a gramophone and supply of records. Went on board in the morning and had dinner there. In the afternoon went over to the bathing beach on the other side of the island, a fine place, with any number of people loafing about in bathing costumes. Explored some caves and chased a family of lizards into a crack. Saw some new varieties of shellfish-like large slaters, of an average length of four to six inches, and with flesh like our limpets; also some young nautilus about 1/4 in. long. Had tea, with strawberries and cream. Got back at 5:30 p.m., and found mate and his wife on board. Went ashore, and had dinner with the boss and played cards. Would far rather have listened to the music, but that couldn't be helped. Turned in at 12:10 a.m.

7th April.—Yesterday the new mate asked the Doc and self to go with him to a meeting tonight. I had to meet him on the club steps at seven. Turned up at seven, waited till 7:45; no mate. Later found second mate, who informed me mate was drunk, and that the bos'n and he had had a scrap, in which Mr. Bos'n knocked him kicking. Good for the old bos'n. So much for him. He'll need to go.

8th April.—Mate did not turn up today at all. Went out to the dockyard and got my windlass parts; no adventures this time. Cheery had found a broken piston and ring in the windlass engine, so that had to be attended to. Had a most excellent Welsh rarebit in the Palm Gardens at 11:30, and then came back to dream of it.

9th April.—Came alongside the quay today about two, having got the windlass fixed; its parts came down yesterday from New York. Took on board our anchor and chain, also fifteen tons of fuel oil in one hundred barrels. Did that in 5-1/4 hours, which was not at all bad. Very hot today. Running about like a blue-faced fly. The boss is quite happy emptying drums of oil and getting in everyone's way. The latest mate turned up this morning and got chased for his life, so we have still one to find.

Moved off from our part of the wharf to another, this time to take in one hundred tons of ballast made up of Bermuda rock, which is very light for its bulk. Hired a parcel of niggers and set them at work to put it on board. Signed off the two new mates. I don't think they would have been of much use, anyhow. Had a great pantomime getting the ship docked here. We dropped anchor too soon, and it appears to have got caught up on something or other. We shall have a job lifting it. I am staying on board again. Warped out a bit and tried to get anchor up; no use, so just came back again. There are thousands of large cockroaches on the dock; I hope they stay there. Took the Doc to the Palm Gardens, and had a somewhat hefty supper consisting of soup, chops, Welsh rarebit and eggs.

11th April.—Finished the ballast. Have a new mate, a Nova Scotian Scot. He's a nut, but I think quite a good seaman. I also signed on skipper's son again as second. Got out again, and had another unsuccessful shot at getting the anchor up. Engaged a diver for first thing tomorrow morning. Got all my accounts checked and paid.

12th April.—Diver arrived at nine, descended to the bottom of the harbour, and with commendable promptitude duly came to the surface and reported that our anchor had secreted itself under the bights of a heavy mooring the Admiralty had been careless with. Gave the aquatic gentleman a rope to make fast to the mooring chain, while we carefully wound the other end round the drum of the winch—and, lo! the anchor was free. Rang full ahead on the main engine and steamed off to outside White's Island. As the Ocean Transport are making a claim for damage to their buoy, which the boss intends to contest, he had the idea this morning of sneaking the ship off to sea before they could seize her. So he hoisted his house flag and the Blue Peter first thing, and then, as the pilot wasn't on board, he spent part of the forenoon blowing the whistle for him. After this had gone on for a bit the Ocean Transport Co.

woke up to the fact that we didn't intend spending next Christmas in Bermuda. They consulted a lawyer and started off to arrest the ship. However, they settled the matter for £50. The new anchor shackles wouldn't fit, so took them to a blacksmith who knocked them about a bit. Captain and I went ashore, finished our business, and came out to the ship on the roof of a ferry.

BOOK III

CHAPTER I

BACK TO RUM ROW

12th April.—Put to sea at 12:30 p.m. Nice breeze outside and making about seven knots. Boss has decided not to go back to New York, as he says they will be waiting for him at the gangway if he does. He was followed down here by 'one in authority.' Flat calm all this morning, and doing about four knots under power. Wind came away from the W. about 11:15, freshened later, so we got all sails on her. Played my Japanese violin, also the concertina, for a bit, and enjoyed the music myself. A fine fresh breeze sprang up in the evening. Was very much surprised to find, on reading the log at 10:30 p.m., that we had done just over eight knots in the last hour. Damned good for this old hooker.

13th April.—Last night's speed was so damn good that this extraordinary ship early repented of her relapse into virtue by carrying away the starboard rigging on the foremast and breaking the gaff on the mainmast. Gaff-guys must have been too slack. This she did at 2:30 a.m. today, rolling so wildly that she threw all the fire-buckets and the rack off the top of the charthouse. That's a new trick; the rack was screwed down by brass screws, but they didn't worry her. About one, the wind shifted a little, so we hoisted the mizzen sail and the head sails, and are now making about five knots.

16th April.—Fine day, but colder as we are now north of the Gulf Stream. The mate is a comedian, and I must try to record some of his stories from time to time. He tells an amusing yarn of how he got out of Barbados. He had left Halifax for Barbados with a small

cargo in an equally small two-masted brig. When he got there, his owners apparently left him stranded. A cargo of scrap metal offered for
Halifax, so he took it. His owners sent him no money, so he paid out
what he had of his own to clear the ship. As that didn't prove enough
by $180, they wouldn't give him his papers. He then looked around,
and managed to get eight innocent people to ship as passengers, charging $40 a skull, but most of that money had to go in buying provisions
for them. So he was still stuck. Got out of it by lining them up and telling
them he would have to take charge of their spare cash in view of the
immigration laws in Nova Scotia. By this means he collected the necessary funds and got his ship away. Two hundred and fifty miles from
Bermuda he struck heavy weather, and lost his rigging and mast
wedges. Also a lot of the food went bad, so he put into St. George. Since
the owners again paid no attention to him, he pawned his chronometer, sextant, telescope and clock. Paid his passengers back, and shipped
with us as mate when the chance offered. That is how he arrived on
this ship, so he says, but I fancy some American magazine is responsible for the yarn. Midday today we were 260 miles off.

18th April.—In soundings. Made our landfall a little to the east of
Fire Inlet, about twelve miles off, so turned to starboard and went off
up the coast. Flat calm. Got off Montauk Point about 4:30, and to our
new anchorage at 6:30, where we dropped anchor in twenty-two fathoms. The *Star* is lying not far from us. Much to my surprise, we made
a sale to a small fishing boat that came to us about 7:30 and took the
large number of five cases of Bisquit brandy away with him in
exchange for what I hope are 125 perfectly good dollars. Wind in the
south and inclined to breeze up a bit. A visitor, the captain of a two-
masted schooner lying near us, says things are absolutely rotten here,
and that he doesn't think there will be any improvement until
September. Took the first watch, i.e., eight till twelve.

It isn't hot up here yet so we have got some of the stoves going
again. It is blowing pretty hard from the south, with rain, looking like
a dirty sort of day. This being Good Friday, the crew are having a holiday and spending it mostly in their bunks. I know that is where I have
been all day, and a dashed good place to be in when you have a rotten sore throat. Mr. Mate is busy making a net to catch clams with;
more power to him!

19th April.—Not much of a day. Still keeping kind of cold. Spent a good part of today sleeping. Ship back at her old rolling tricks again. We had visitors this morning in the shape of the captain and two others off a two-masted schooner lying near us. We shall have to start returning calls one of these days. On watch twelve to four, so turned in early.

20th April.—Sunday, still cold. Divine service in bed, and a good place it is for it. Morrison and Peters have started a laundry forward, and are charging 3s. per dozen for any kind of articles. The ship, I may say, supplies the soap, while the sea supplies the water. They ought to make quite a good thing of it as they are full up with orders today. I have sent them my engineroom trousers, along with other articles. The cutter was out today and got two captives, one of them a motor-boat that came from the *Star*. The other started off to make out to sea, but the cutter fired a shot at him that brought him back in a hurry. No sign of any communication from the shore, so far. Cold and dull.

21st April.—Busy today. Polished all the woodwork in the cabin with O'Cedar polish. Looks well now. The others are bending a new wire backstay to the foremast. Two Dutchmen from Nova Scotia were in tonight, trying to get some tobacco. Gave them, or rather sold them, some Honest and 200 Gold Flake. They are going to bring me over some canned clams, which we shall use for bait. One got fairly 'fou,' and, as they have a mile's row back to their ship in the dark and it's fairly choppy, he'll need to mind his feet. A bit warmer tonight.

22nd April.—I wouldn't have had the poor old cook's job today for a small fortune. The language from the galley has been a perfect revelation. Strong south wind is blowing and a big swell is getting up. The galley is full of steam from pots which carefully unloaded their contents into the fire. One roll ejected the mess-boy in a heap into the alleyway, with half a dozen pots and a baking-tin full of dough in wild pursuit. As cook can only fill his pots one-third full, the cooking is somewhat slow and meal-times are elastic. The *Star* got anchor up at three this afternoon and steamed off to sea. Good!

If there is business here, that's an opponent gone. While on watch this morning I saw a magnificent display of lightning from the bridge. One flash struck the steel foremast, but it did no harm, merely passing through the ship into the water. Was absolutely blinded for about half an hour. Now came the snag. Looking at the after compass later in the day, I found it appeared to be about 90° out. Went on the bridge and took a bearing by the steering compass on Montauk, which we can just see. Found it out about the same. It's a good thing we are at anchor and likely to remain so quite long enough to let the compasses settle down again. Captain knows nothing about compass adjustment, nor does the mate, and, as all I know is from reading Captain Lecky, we will leave Flinders bars and magnets alone. Our next port should be Halifax, so with any luck— as we shall only be out of sight of land for a few hours while crossing the entrance to the Bay of Fundy—it won't matter.

23rd April.—Rolling in a diabolical way nearly all day. She has now managed to roll all the wire-seizings on the main rigging loose, and it is sagging like anything. The hard wood blocks that the stays pass over at the crosstrees are worn through and the wire is now chafing on the edge of a steel plate. Doc demanded his breakfast in bed this morning, and got it; damned nonsense that will be put a stop to very quickly. I can see us running short of fresh vegetables before long, as yesterday a sea washed two bags of potatoes and some onions and carrots over the side. They were perched on No. 2 hatch, where they should have been safe. Getting warmer again. Wind has died down. A three-master joined us today, the one that we spoke to when leaving in December, and again when we gave her coal and water in February. On watch tonight from eight to twelve. I shall take the concertina up to the charthouse and do some practising. Carried out the above-mentioned threat, and gave Peters a lesson in concertina playing in exchange for which he made me an excellent sandwich and a cup of tea, thus returning good for evil.

24th April.—Today started considerably earlier than I care for, inasmuch as 8 a.m. is Christian-like, but 12:30 a.m. is not. I was just turning in off watch when I heard a motor engine near. I went on deck to look with practically nothing on, and found a big boat nearly alongside. There appeared to be a lot of men on board, so I raced back for my revolver and trousers. However, there was no need for alarm as it was Hamman's boat. His brother is now with us and a very decent fellow. He sleeps on the settee in the mate's room. Sent off 300 cases, which is a start. They have 120 miles to go with it this time, so we won't see them again for at least three days. Spent a good part of the day in bed, as I have a rotten chill, and did myself proud as far as hot toddy was concerned in the evening. About ten this morning Mr. Mate, second mate, and three others set off in the starboard lifeboat on a round of visits to some other schooners. At 10:30 tonight they returned, after adventures so varied and peculiar that it is a wonder half of them got back at all. They had dinner on one boat and tea on another. The second visit appears to have developed into a pure scrap. Mate's a quarrelsome devil in drink and as strong as a bull. He got mad and chased the youngster all over the place, had him hunted up the rigging and out on the jib boom; in fact, put the wind up him so properly that finally the lad ran to the cook for protection. The captain of the ship had to take Mr. Mate by the hair of the head and beat some sort of sense into him. They all got back much more by luck than good guidance.

25th April.—A summer-like day, very warm with bright sunshine. A sample, I hope, of what we may expect in the future. Spent a good part of the time trimming cargo and ballast. Yesterday's picnic party are not in the best of form—at least, two members of it are not. Got the main rigging all fixed up; it's thrapped into the mast, giving a sort of tight-laced appearance to a respectable main mast. So now all that remains to be done is to repair the main gaff and we are a ship again. Wish I could get rid of this cold of mine.

26th April.—Cook very much under the weather and unable to cook any dinner, so that the mess-boy had to turn to and do his work, and did it quite well. During the afternoon the mate suggested I should compose a 'Bootleggers' March' for the pipes, so in the evening I sought inspiration and have got something down on paper. Discussed matters of international importance with Cheery for an hour in the evening. Turned in at 10:15.

27th April.—Expected a boat out last night, but had no luck. It was calm enough in all conscience. This is going to be a long, long job by all appearances. Another A1 day, part of which we spent fishing. Second mate got a nice cod. Had visitors in the shape of some 'Scandehouvians,' as the mate calls them. They were out fishing and had some mussels. We got some from them, as the fish here object to salt pork as bait. The supercargo was with them and stayed to dinner with us. Quite a decent chap.

28th April.—On watch from twelve till four this morning. Beautiful dawn and very warm. Spent nearly all day fishing, and landed a 10-lb. haddock and, a 48-lb. skate, which took some pulling in. Then I got a curious fish called a 'puffer.' When it is laid on its back and its belly is smartly beaten with a piece of wood it swells up to an enormous size, and when put in a bucket of water it can't sink. Got a big cod also. About four the wind went into the S.E. and started to blow a bit; but the glass has fallen very little. Hamman's brother is wondering how much of a blow is coming. Feeling sleepy tonight. Cold getting better. Tried over my 'March to Rum Row,' for the pipes; with a few alterations, it will not be bad—at least, that is the composer's opinion.

A NEW ARRIVAL ON RUM ROW

READY FOR DELIVERY

CHAPTER II

SLACK BUSINESS

29 April.—The conditions on shore must be extraordinary so far as this prohibition law is concerned: for instance, Hamman the Second told us today that he and two others have a small restaurant not far off Broadway, into which a good deal of our stuff finds its way. The other night they were running a load of 150 cases in a motor furniture van and were going to put it in the cellar of the restaurant. The driver had instructions to put up at a garage just outside New York and come in in the early morning when things were quiet, and when there would be a friendly cop on the beat. However, when the van got to this garage the driver was given the tip that the Federals were going to have a look round that night, so off they went and arrived outside the restaurant when supper was in full blast and the street as busy as could be. "What happened?" we asked him. "Well," he said, "just to let you see what our average citizen thinks of this Volstead Act, what happened was this. We handed the cases across the sidewalk, and every person supping inside helped pass them to the cellar by forming a chain, same as you do here. We got every blessed one in without any interference, even with the traffic cop at the corner looking on."

30th April.—Another good day, though the glass keeps curiously low. We have managed to lose the balance of our bait, so I am afraid fishing is going to be 'na poo' until we manage to get some more. Tried the 'murderer,' but so far that has yielded no results. Some boats were out in the afternoon, but for other people. One came to us, but the price we shouted out to them was evidently too high, for they smiled sweetly and went elsewhere. Our boat arrived at seven, and got 319 this time, which is better than nothing. Hamman's brother has had enough of the *Cask*, and went off ashore, but has left a compatriot, and, as he is a seaman (at least he was in the American Navy during the war), we shall probably have him with us for a little longer than the others. On watch eight to twelve midnight. At eleven the bos'n was washing clothes in a bucket in the alleyway outside the galley, when some big swells arrived up and she rolled wildly for a few minutes, managing to scatter the bos'n's shirts, etc., all over the shop. One shirt departed at full speed into the donkey-room amongst the coal and had to be rewashed. Bos'n was a happy and pleased man for a bit, judging by his remarks. Our boat forgot our fresh meat, etc., so we shall have to wait for a bit yet. Heard that the *Star* has been captured in Maine, but the papers don't say much about it. It appears she is in St. John, New Brunswick. I don't see that they can do much to her there.

30th April.—Not such a bad day. Compasses nearly back to normal this morning. Spent the forenoon in No. 1 hold shifting cargo. About 2,000 cases that were shifted to make room for the ballast had been laid over everything else, and had all to be put back in No 2 again. Slept all the afternoon. Tea consisted of salt ling fish and rice, with a little Bird's custard powder, so we imagined we were eating *Kedgeree a l'Indienne*. A small dose of curry powder was added, to supply the *Indienne* part of it. The *Alaska*, a small trawler that pups for the *Star*, came up this afternoon. During our game we heard a steamer blowing, and found the *Star* back again, which means the cutter will be out now, as they watch her. They didn't detain her very long in St. John, New Brunswick. Tomorrow the first of May, and we have only managed to get rid of 8,700 cases, although it is eight months since we started. Blowing a bit tonight and raining hard. S.E. wind. Glass falling. Gave some washing to the firm of Morrison, Peters & Co., Ltd.; my engineroom shirt this time, which has several months of oil and dirt on it, so they have a bit of a job ahead of them.

1st May.—Last night, after I had written up the day's log; we had what is known locally as a Jersey squall. About midnight the wind suddenly increased to something approaching a tornado, accompanied by torrential rain and very vivid flashes of lightning. These squalls are supposed to last about quarter of an hour, but this one forgot he was a Jersey squall and lasted about two hours. Turned in when the glass showed signs of rising. However, I was wakened at 5:30 a.m. by three oil drums that had broken adrift and were trying to batter my bulkhead in, making a deuce of a row. We rolled heavily all day, but the weather is clearing and the sun is out again. Had a sleep in the afternoon for a little. Got a new game for the evenings. I get the gramophone going and sit up in my bunk and accompany the singers on my Japanese violin. I rather fancy it does not improve the melodiousness of the song. Made a splendid mess in the mate's room—at least a jar of strawberry jam did. I was peacefully playing the concertina, when the ship took a lurch which sent me flying up against the side, and the glass jar of jam on to the floor. Our old friend with the cork leg turned up tonight at 11:30. It was a job getting him on board, as there is a big swell still. He went off with 18 cases and will be back again soon, he says. We all admire that chap; it's no joke coming out eighteen miles in a wee open boat alone. Beautiful night, without a breath of wind. Have the graveyard watch tonight.

2nd May.—Spent most of my watch yarning with the bos'n and drinking tea to keep myself awake. Heard a motorboat about 3 a.m., and tried to get him to come over to us by signalling with the Morse lamp, but there was nothing doing. The *Star* went off out to sea this morning, and the *Alaska*, her pup, followed this afternoon. A new cutter, the *Acushnet*, came round and inspected us today. He took our photograph, so I took his. Breeze has sprung up again, so I am afraid we shall see no boats out tonight, and not much chance of any till Monday evening, as the lazy blighters won't work on Saturdays or Sundays. I should get some mail when the next boat comes out.

3rd May.—Slept all the forenoon. I don't know why, but I am getting very sleepy-headed. I think it must be the atmosphere in the saloon. Captain is in his bunk at all hours of the day and night and smokes bad cigars. Put in some hefty work at the Japanese violin for an hour in the afternoon, and was rather surprised at the volume of tone that the instrument gave out after I had bound it round with a piece of copper wire. In the evening there was a noisy card party in the saloon, so I adjourned to the second engineer's room till it was over, when we had a small concert until 10 p.m. He sang, while I played his accompaniments on the one-stringed affair. Since pumping up the sixty ton forward ballast tank, the ship is a good deal more steady and comfortable. Mr. Mate would talk the hind-legs off a wheelbarrow, and it's all about himself. It doesn't matter what the topic is, he has had some experience of the subject under discussion. The limit was reached today at dinner-time when we were discussing death, and he chimed in with the remark, 'Death isn't so bad. I have gone through it three times now.' This turned out to mean he had three times lost consciousness in the water.

4th May.—Sunday, beautiful day. The other ships lying here had boats off to them, so it's funny our gentleman can't manage to get out to us. I think things must have been going wrong ashore since the boss is no longer there to watch what's doing.

5th May.—My birthday, and the thirty seventh at that. Getting on towards middle age, and, as far as I can see, without much more sense than I had at the age of seven—if I had I wouldn't be here. Busy morning. Took the saloon settee to pieces, beat the cushions thoroughly, and mended them where the sewing had given way at the seams. Had a game of skittles with hatch wedges in the evening, Cheery and self playing the chief engineer and mate, and losing seven to two. The chief is now engaged in designing a deck golf course, though what sort of a game we will get out of that the Lord alone knows. No boats, though eight passed us.

6th May.—Another boatless day. I think something must have gone very far wrong ashore. Someone with malice aforethought managed to get a couple of bottles into the fo'c'sle this afternoon; result, a certain amount of rowdiness. Second mate was nearly mad—in fact, for a bit he was mad—throwing knives at the mess-boy and indulging an idle fancy in various ways of that description, until he was forcibly restrained. Mr. Mate had more sense; he went straight to his bunk and turned in. The mess-boy's face is considerably scarred owing to this afternoon's amusement. Turned in at 10:30.

7th May.—Dull today and a bit cold. Several are suffering from 'the day after the night before' feeling, and there is no sign of anything doing from the shore. Finished a water-colour I was working on, and gave it to the second engineer.

CHAPTER III

FISHING AND FOOD

8th May.—We've been here three weeks now, and only sent 623 cases over the side, which is the blessed limit. Glass falling, and inclined to blow up a bit from the east. Caught a large edition of the fish I described on the 28th April. It belongs to the breed of 'angler fish,' and above its mouth is a fishing-rod with a small leaf-like finger at the end, which is the bait. It weighs about 45 lbs. and is an ugly-looking brute, very slimy and jelly-fish-like. Cook is raging wild today. The mess-boy had removed one of the safety-bars off the range, and a pot of boiling water took charge. There will be something approaching murder in the galley yet.

9th May.—Woke to find a dirty day in full working order, with half a gale from E.N.E. and heavy rain squalls. Read, slept and meditated. Cook managed to amuse himself for a bit by putting a sack on the back of the angler fish, sitting on it, and tobogganing about the deck in great style. All he had to do was to sit still, as the slime of the fish and the rolling of the ship did the rest. Did so much sleeping that I am afraid I shan't do much tonight. On watch tomorrow from four to eight. This breeze has scattered the fleet, and only three of us are left. The others are cruising about in case they carry away their last anchors, I expect. I jammed the angler fish's mouth open with a hatch wedge and took his photograph.

10th May.—Weather much improved; wind away and glass rising. Overhauled my stores and found more than I had expected, for which I am not sorry. I can see a certain amount of trouble ahead, as the second engineer is decidedly in the bad graces of the chief. Doc sides, I suppose, with the chief, and hasn't spoken to the second for four days. I don't know what it's about, but it's the effect of lying at anchor, I think. At seven a boat came straight for us. Everyone's spirits rose, but we had no luck. She only came near enough to enquire if we knew where the *Star* was lying. Directed him, and off he went into the mist to look for her. One of the crew asked if the boss was on board. Don't know who he was.

11th May.—Our fresh vegetables are down to about three stone of potatoes and a few carrots and turnips. Weather still cold, with the wind in the east, and no appearance of it shifting at present. Our Yankee who is on board was a disappointed man when he saw the boat go off elsewhere yesterday. He had visions of beef-steaks at home today, with the result that he has taken to his bunk, or rather the settee in the mate's room, and absolutely refuses to budge out of it. I also lay up most of the day.

12th May.—Had a job with cook this morning. When eight bells went there was no sign of breakfast. His cabin was locked, and, after bashing in the ventilator, we saw him lying stark naked on the concrete floor. We burst in the door and found him stiff with cold and quite unconscious. However, we took it in relays to rub him with raw rum, and after about two hours of this he came round, and we left him well wrapped up in warm blankets. He is now—6 p.m.—feeling not so bad, but it was a near thing for him. We'll give him full marks for making soup; I believe he could make good stock out of the staves of an empty salt-pork barrel. Wild morning; very heavy rain squalls. A weird craft of Hamman's brought out his assistant Maloney and a Mr. Lorne, who knows the agent at home and in the boss's absence is representing him ashore, with orders to keep in touch with me. He brought a message to shift up close to New York, which will bring us into calmer waters. A careful man is Lorne: he had his letter in the sole of his boot. The boss at present is living at the end of a fishing rod somewhere in Nova Scotia. Thank goodness for a mail at last. I got nine letters.

13th May.—Had the usual job getting up the anchor, which took about two hours, with the windlass leaking steam at every joint. It was a beautiful day, with a very heavy swell coming in from the S.E. We are doing about 5 knots, and, as we have a hundred miles to go, we should get to Ambrose about eight o'clock tomorrow morning.

CHAPTER IV

ON NEW GROUND

14th May.—Got up to what we think is our new ground at 7:30 a.m. and dropped anchor. Saw the *Berengaria* passing about five miles inshore. There are five other boats here, but apparently they are pups off a steamer, for three of them were alongside the mother ship getting supplies when we arrived; then they went off to pastures new. Had a visit from a strange Revenue cutter.

15th May.—Up at four, as I was on watch. Did some fishing, and landed another large angler fish. It was a bit of a job getting him over the rail single-handed, but managed it with the aid of the net the mate had made to catch clams.

16th May.—Everyone cursing and grumbling.

17th May.—Another strange cutter was nosing round today. At eleven I took one of the boats and started off to pay some calls, with the object of trying to get some paraffin. First I went over to the *Maryville*, a steamer lying near us, with a large schooner on either side of her. She left home with 95,000 cases at the beginning of last December, and is practically finished. She had a very dirty passage coming over, taking 33 days and 20 hours to make this place. She has lost four anchors and five hundred fathoms of cable altogether. When a full-powered steamer does that, there are excuses for the poor old *Cask*. The captain was a decent old chap, at present covered with boils. They have three supers on board, one of them a lad from Glasgow who is going to return my call and wishes to try the bagpipes. He is a keen highlander, and we appear to have a good many mutual friends and acquaintances. Got back with three small drums of paraffin in time for dinner. In the afternoon I decided to visit an auxiliary schooner about 2 miles in the opposite direction. Got on board and yarned to the super there, while Mr. Mate, who came with us, went down and interviewed the captain, with a view to whisky, which was forthcoming. They have had their trials and tribulations also, inasmuch as they too have lost four anchors. At present the flywheel of the engine is in pieces and they are busy fitting a new one. Also, there is only one blade left on their propeller, so they're in fine trim. Chief engineer and the Doc came with us. They retired to the oily regions, and stayed there most of the time. Not a very easy job separating our mate from the ship. The captain, being a Colquhoun from Glasgow, knows all the pubs our chief engineer knows, so they peregrinated together in imagination. I couldn't leave without a drink, so had one, and then managed to induce Mr. Mate to come on board the boat. Rowing back, we passed close to the cutter, and gave him a cheery wave, to which all on board replied. We are quite good friends with the cutters and always get a wave from them; *not always from the bridge*, though, but sometimes. As long as we are not lying too near any shipping that is suspected of carrying more than honest-to-God whisky they don't bother us. If only our shore connection had been better we would have been finished long ago. Glass falling, wind rising from the N.W. Our ill-gotten gains amounted to ten gallons of paraffin. Our stonemason A.B., who had part of the roof of an hotel fall on him, made rather an amusing remark today—one of his daft ones. The bos'n was washing down the poop, and he was getting water up in a bucket from the port side. He was in the way of the brush gang, so the bos'n said to him, "Go over to the starboard side, you and your magenta bucket." "All right," he replied quite seriously, "but is there any water over there?"

Skipper and I had a confab., and decided to move off about seven miles nearer the Ambrose Lightship and about due S. of Long Beach. There is nothing doing here. Got steam up at two, and by three, with the usual trouble, the anchor was up. Motored along W. by N. for an hour and ten minutes and then dropped anchor, again in fourteen fathoms. Can't see any fleet, though there are supposed to be 26 or 27 boats about. We are in the track of the big ships, so on thick nights we shall have to keep our eyes skinned and the bell going over time. Boat hailed us at 11:15 p.m., but they were also looking for the fleet. Fireworks on shore; could see the rockets.

19th May.—Got steam up about 11 a.m. and started to heave in the anchor. You would think that we couldn't do any harm over a simple job like heaving up an anchor well out in the Atlantic. But we could and did. When the anchor came to the surface it brought one of the Atlantic cables with it, and we had a bit of a job freeing it. Managed to tear about a foot of insulation away, so as it was no use to us, we put it back where it belonged. Came about seven miles in a south westerly direction. Dropped anchor in fourteen fathoms again, near the *Vincent*, which was in Glasgow with us. No sign of anything doing so far as we are concerned, but other boats are doing a good business, though at what figure I don't know. Schooners and steamers are at anchor in all directions as far as we can see. I counted twenty-seven craft this morning. Hamman's man is getting more fed up every day.

20th May.—Had our first indication of business. In the forenoon a boat came alongside, threw us his rope, and enquired the price. I said twenty-one dollars, to which his reply was curt but convincing: "Cast off that bloody rope." He said he could buy at eighteen, and went off, presumably to do so. Had hardly turned in when there was a shout of a boat. Two fellows came on board. One of them showed me his order slip:

> Champagne $23
> Rye $21
> Scotch $17

That was only for small lots, and I don't know what people are paying for large amounts. At these figures the game is absolutely finished so far as any profit to us is concerned. Don't know what we are to do. If I go as low as that without instructions in writing from the boss, someone will turn round and ask, "What about the other dollars?" It was raining a bit tonight. The *Olympic* passed fairly near us today, but too far off for photographing.

21st May.—Spent part of the day experimenting with a mixture of fuel oil and paraffin for our riding lights, two parts fuel to one part paraffin.

Captain wants to make paraffin an excuse to make for Halifax, and was not over-delighted with our success. Cigarettes have been finished for some time now. Pipes are mostly in evidence, but some hardy spirits are smoking newspaper rolled round shredded plug and say it is excellent, though don't look as though they thought it was. Made a pipe out of a hard wood hatch wedge, but I hope I shan't have to smoke it. Turned in at 10:30 after a yarn on the bridge with the Doc on the advisability of his going ashore to see what is the matter.

22nd May.—Boats out to everyone but us. There must be something serious going on. I shall try to get some letters ashore tomorrow via the three-masted schooner that is lying near us, and also see if they can spare us any cigarettes or decent tobacco. A large two-funnelled steamer passed, apparently having at some time been gutted by fire, in charge of a big tug.

While I was on watch tonight I got a pleasant surprise. A big boat came to us at 11:30 p.m., and I argued and bargained for a bit with him. He wouldn't give more than seventeen to begin with, but I finally got him up to $18.50, at which price he took 150 cases. I think, and hope, I have obtained a regular customer, as he says he is coming back tomorrow night on the strength of that. I have ordered cigarettes and papers.

23rd May.—Nothing much doing today. Painting masts and odd little things like that. Fine all day. Everyone bad-tempered. There was a fight in the fo'c'sle which was stopped with a fire extinguisher. Wind started to rise about three. Moderate breeze at six, with a sea choppy enough to make it very doubtful if any boats will be out tonight.

CHAPTER V

CUTTERS AND HIJACKERS

24th May.—Very stormy all day, with a three-quarters gale from the south and a heavy thunderstorm between eight and nine. The lightning was very vivid and near. Chief engineer and mate had words. I can see Mr. Mate getting a smashed face one of these days.

25th May.—A beautiful day and quite warm. Got a surprise at breakfast time when a boat arrived out with our American naval friend back again. I hadn't expected to see him any more. He brought fresh instructions to move, but, as neither he nor his instructions knew where we were to go, we decided to stay where we are. Also, and more important, he brought out four hundred cigarettes. This fellow Lewis says Hamman & Co. intend to start unloading us tomorrow night with three boats. Personally, ' I hae ma doots.' A small cutter was watching us all day and all night.

26th May.—Cutter stayed out all last night and put a stop to any business. This has been the warmest day we have had yet. Spent part of the afternoon clearing the speaking-tube from the bridge to the engineroom. It goes down through No. 3 hold, and it contained at least two gallons of water, so no wonder it would only gurgle. Ping Pong gave me a hand. Had a piece of excitement at 11:15, just as I was turning in. Shouts of "Boat;" got up and found a small one alongside, to which I gave eighteen cases for $320, which allowed $4 discount. As I was receiving the cash, along came another boat. "Things are moving," says I. So they were. There had been three cutters out here all afternoon, the most we had yet seen at a time.

One of them suddenly bore down on us, and it was a case of scatter, the buyer of the second boat being left on board. He and I were discussing things when—bang! boom!—the cutter was firing at his pal's. With the searchlight full on, it looked very like one of Matania's fanciful drawings in the *Illustrated London News* during the war. The motorboat stopped at the third shot and came alongside the cutter. We saw no more of him for a bit. I was wondering if his buyer was going to be marooned with us for some time, perhaps days. However, about two hours later back he came for his pal. The cutter had searched him and his boat, but finding no money or any documents, let him go. They wanted at first to take in a load, but I advised them not to, and it was as well I did so, for they hadn't been gone three minutes before the cutter was round again with searchlight playing and gave us a thorough examination.

27th May.—Bos'n was in a humorous mood after dinner and gave us some imitations of Chinese singing, with the idea of annoying Ping Pong. They were very like an imitation we had once before from him of a baboon he had been shipmates with. Ate our last ham for dinner, and discovered a bag of haricot beans, which I had thought were peas. They were very good with tinned butter and vinegar out of a pickle jar.

28th May.—Skipper is getting very restive. I think continual badly cooked salt horse is getting on his nerves. It was very misty early, and we had our bell going as a steamer was blowing near us. It cleared up a little later and was quite warm; no wind, swell, rolling a bit. Hamman, I think, doesn't intend to take any more from us. The other ships here are getting boats regularly; the *Vincent* had four today. No fish here, apparently—at least we can't get any of them. Morrison told me tonight of a ship he was on taking a large bronze statue of a Highland soldier on board in Antwerp. It had been cast in Germany, and they brought it to Glasgow. So that's where some of our war memorials come from.

29th May.—In the afternoon I went over and visited the *Vincent*, with several letters, and got the skipper to agree to send them ashore for me. She's a fine boat. Stayed on board about an hour, and was back in time for tea. Our provisions are running very low. We haven't any more than twelve or fourteen days of flour at the outside. Then it's hard biscuits. Our American friend, when he came back from his last trip ashore, brought two hams, somewhat expensive ones, as the charge for the boat that brought him out was $100. Got several boats tonight. I had a row with one fellow who wanted about a dozen bottles as samples. Sold him 60 cases. Another took 85, and I had no difficulty in getting $18. Then another bold lad came, but he wanted to buy at $16. Nothing doing. As this one was leaving, a very large boat, something like one of our M.L.'s, came up alongside, with at least a dozen men on board. Fortunately, our deck was full of men, as I fancy he was up to monkey tricks. He went off after examining us. These fellows will attack a drunk or sleeping ship, but don't like risking their hides. When these big boats come near us we watch them like hawks. I have a blue flare ready on the bridge to attract attention. Also, none of the officers go on deck unarmed at night. There's too much money in this ship for my liking. Several raids have been carried out, actually by one of the partners in a rumrunner. One boat about five miles east of us was raided not long ago. One partner was on board as supercargo, the other doing the shore end. The shore end lad had a raid carried out and cleared off after with, I am told, about $40,000.

31st May.—Today started well. At 2 a.m. a boat came and took 30 cases at $18—fifteen Old Smuggler and fifteen Sandy Mac. Managed to get four cigarettes from a fellow on one of the boats who comes from Possilpark, and he promised to bring out a carton or two. Am much afraid Hamman has given us up; we've had no sign of him, or Lorne either, for nearly a fortnight. Good business tonight. One lad took 100, so I gave him one to himself; another took 75, another 40. This last carefully broke all his cases open and put the bottles into bags for buoying purposes, if chased. It's a good notion. The sacks, each containing half a dozen bottles, are tied together a few yards apart on a long rope. Then, should a cutter or Customs boat give chase, they dump the lot overboard with a small bladder on the end of the rope to buoy it.

Later on they come back and collect their nefarious purchases. There is a good deal of what is known as 'hijacking,' inshore and out here too; in plain English, 'highway robbery.' Our last customer left at 4 a.m.

CHAPTER VI

MORE VISITORS

2nd June.—Nothing doing all day. Cheery, our second engineer, found two packets of cigarette-papers in the pocket of an old suit, so I have ceased making cigarettes out of toilet paper for a day or two. No boats today, though some passed near us. A three-masted schooner was towed up to-day by the *Vincent*'s pup and is made fast to the *Vincent*'s stern. She has shoved up two very strong cargo lights, and, with her white hull, looks not unlike the cutter. She will scare everything for miles. We shall require to leave here in a day or two now if food doesn't arrive.

3rd June.—The same as yesterday. No word from shore. Chief has got the engineroom looking very well indeed, as he has spent several very busy days graining paint. Bos'n says he is ill, but comes aft for his tot all the same. The cutter was round this forenoon and captured one motorboat, but sent it inshore. It's quite a game: if the cutter has been in one spot too long, a boat comes out and gets itself captured. The cutter then takes it inshore, and his pals do a brisk business for two or three hours. Today they will be disappointed, as the *Gresham* did not go inshore with her capture. Glass dropping, raining a little in the evening. On watch eight till twelve tonight.

4th June.—Very wet last night. All the same, I got rid of 100 cases. I should hear from Hamman very soon now if he is going to do anything. We decided to send the Doc ashore tomorrow if no word comes out tonight. He is quite pleased with the idea. I fancy he sees a bit of a skite ahead of him. If he goes I hope he won't skite too much. At present his room looks rather peculiar. His roof is leaking and he has cotton wool fastened to the planking with adhesive tape, giving the roof a wounded appearance. More stuff away tonight, about 140 cases.

5th June.—Very misty all day—in fact, more or less thick fog. Had our bell going at regular intervals. It was rather eerie, with steamer whistles and ships' bells all round us and nothing to be seen. One boat came enquiring what we had and our prices. Says he can buy Benedictine at $17. We shall see. At last, just when we were at our last gasp, Hamman's people have arrived with stores. The Doc is very disappointed, as his trip is cancelled. My offer of seventeen to Hamman has borne fruit. He says he will unload us before the end of this month. Letters from the other side. I can see the shareholders are doing some worrying, and I don't wonder.

6th June.—Up all last night. The boats kept arriving at inconveniently spaced intervals and only taking small quantities. A perfect day, the most summer-like we have had yet, and very warm. About eight this evening our first boat came out, and went off with 50 cases. It had become very hot and muggy, and at about ten thunder came over from the N.W. It was the best display we have had for some time. For about half an hour we had a wild storm, one flash seeming to go into the water about twenty yards from the ship's side. About ten minutes later the wind came, a real Jersey squall this time. During the wind the lightning never ceased. The storm died down at 11:30 p.m., and at 3 a.m. another boat took 35. Then, at 6 a.m., out comes an old friend, who took 25 White Horse and smashed the cases up and put them in bags. The deck looks like the yard of a joiner's shop.

7th June.—Saturday, spent most of the forenoon humping cases out of the holds. We have fifty of nearly everything on deck. The seas don't come over the bulwarks now, so they won't wash overboard as they did last December. No. 1 hold is full of coal dust, and I got so filthy that I had to have a sponge bath. The *Vincent*—bad luck to her!—went off about 2:30 this afternoon. Last night I heard a boat hail her, ask for the *Cask*, and be told we were off to the S.W. Result, we lost the boat. I believe the *Maryville* is away now also. Bos'n has been having one of his cheery spells and has been invisible for four days now. However, he is about today, though looking somewhat under the weather. Second mate has been asking to get ashore, and is sulking because skipper won't let him. The cutter came out this after noon and stayed with us. During the night one boat came, a big cabin cruiser. She has 600 h.p. on board and can do thirty-five knots. Thought she was after White Horse from what someone shouted, but when I got the 'queer fellow' down to the saloon it turned out to be 'White's Alcohol' he was after.

8th June.—Sunday, had an old friend back at 8 p.m., but, as the cutter was about, he lay well off for an hour or so till the cutter showed signs of sheering off. Sold him 40 cases.

9th June.—Had our first boat at 9:45 at night. The cutter was about, but evidently looking for something else as he paid no attention. This fellow took 150 cases, and left what I hope are 2,550 perfectly good dollars behind him. Hamman's boat arrived at last with the mail and took 103 cases 'A' mixture of all brands. He went off while we got it on deck, but came back later. Meanwhile another old friend came out for 130, which we gave him. Saw a motorboat on fire in the distance, making quite a big blaze. Hope the fellows are all right; it burned for about forty minutes. Made enquiries tonight about this 'White's Alcohol.' That's what is cutting out our stuff ashore. The finished product goes principally to the 'speakeasies,' as they are called, and the lower dives, and must be rank poison. The fellow who told me added that I could get sent out to me from shore the cases, corks, labels, capsules and bottles of any of the well-known brands, and put what I liked in the bottles and he would dispose of it—of course not paying good Scotch prices of $17 to $18.50. He says there are two small steamers further out who are playing this game. However, I told him I would have nothing to do with that sort of business. We have the reputation of having nothing but the best stuff, and we'll keep it at that.

10th June.—About 2:30 a boat arrived containing Dick, who is an old friend. He had obtained two beautiful black eyes in some scrap on shore that he doesn't remember. They had robbed some lobster-pots on the way out and had a sackful of small lobsters and crabs. We cooked them for him and went fifty-fifty. One of the cutters stood by and watched the loading, but didn't interfere. Another boat came and took 30. Dick took 5; he stayed on board about an hour and ate his ill-gotten gains. So did we. We had quite a busy night. One lad took 150, another 70, so things are moving a wee bit, but not fast enough, all the same.

11th June.—There was a rare row last night between the skipper and the cook. One stood inside and the other outside the galley casting reflections on the authenticity of each other's ancestry and making numerous observations relative to their parents' occupations. About eleven tonight Maloney arrived out along with Lorne. He took 150 and was loaded to the gunwale at that. Lorne stayed, as I didn't like to send him ashore with $30,000 in a loaded boat and that was about the amount I had for him to bank.

12th June.—Lorne had to make a special journey to Halifax to the boss to persuade him to lower his price to $18 even. He has got an offer to discharge the whole at $15 from one of the big corporations who promise to take it in a week, starting with a first load of 2,500 to see if the stuff is good. We would go back to Block Island if that comes off. Lorne has cabled the boss about it. No letters from home this time.

13th June.—Two boats this morning. My impertinent friend, who has calmed down a bit, and another. They took 80. Feeling damned sleepy, as I had no sleep at all last night. Maloney and his usual mob arrived, bringing their cargo back. Captain Ireland, a deaf fellow who carries about one of these electric ear-trumpets, got very drunk going ashore and upset the goods, dinghy and every one going through the surf. They only got 35 cases ashore, so we have 115 back which we didn't expect. Up till midnight we had got rid of 302 cases and had had several new customers. One fellow who took 60 cases had a very fast boat—a twelve cylinder 400 h.p. liberty engine, which he claims will do forty-six knots. We asked him to let us see him going all out, so he went off about one hundred yards and came back at full speed, and passed us doing about thirty-nine to forty. As he is an old friend of the mate's, I promised to keep him one case of champagne.

We had boats at intervals all night, long intervals, so I don't get any sleep between them. Lorne is using my bunk, and as the second engineer was on watch from twelve until four, I lay down in his. Just as I was getting over there was a bang like a gun over my head which brought me up again. It was another boat. The weather just now is ideal, an oil calm. I calculate we have 8,700 cases still on board. We shifted our position a bit, as we were only 11-1/2 miles from Rockaway. It is almost certain that the authorities here are going to pull in a ship from under the twelve-mile limit and make a test case of it, and there is no use being the said test case.

14th June.—Maloney arrived out about 5 p.m. with a letter from Hamman, who says he will unload us in four weeks. I wonder how many more promises he will make. Also he wants the gin at $13, which is a bit low, I think. I got Lorne off about six with $39,700 in his pockets. I hope he manages to get in safely, and I think he was glad to go. It's a mercy the bunch on his boat don't suspect he has £8,000 on him, or he would never get in alive.

CHAPTER VII

THE LADY BOOTLEGGER

16th June.—Shout of "Boat coming." I was sitting on an upturned bucket on No. 2 hatch splicing a rope sling, when I heard the shout. I went up on the bridge, and away in the distance could make out the usual fan of white denoting the approach of a speed boat. Is she coming to us, or will she sheer off and go elsewhere? That's always the question we ask ourselves. "Bet you twenty cigarettes, Mr. Mac, she comes here," shouted the chief, who had just emerged from the engineroom and was standing on the poop watching her. "Right, take you," I replied.

Jumping jings! There's a woman on board, and a child!

There was no time for further speculation, for she came up fast, slowed down, and stopped a few feet off.

We threw her a rope, which she made fast in the bow, and floated quietly against our fenders. All eyes were on the lady, who was dressed in a bathing costume and had a sugar-bag tied round her waist like a kilt. What is more, she was a dashed pretty girl of about twenty-five. The mechanic was Dick, our friend with the two black eyes. The kiddie was a dark-eyed, wee girl about ten.

We threw our monkey-ladder over the side, and madam came up like a lamplighter. "Which of you guys is the supercargo?"

I modestly admitted that I was.

"What ya got?"

I detailed what we had on board, and asked her how much she wanted.

"Say! I want thirty cases of good stuff, and I'll pay $18 and not a cent more. Dick says you are a regular guy and I'll get the proper goods on this ship."

My breath was slowly coming back to me. Out of the whole crowd of us there was only one self-possessed individual, and that was the lady.

"Look here," I said, "everything on this ship is as it left the distilleries in Scotland, and I'll give you my word that nothing has been tampered with. You can break open any case you like and take out a bottle and taste it."

"Nix to that! I'll take yours and Dick's word."

"Right oh, then, we will get the business part squared up; but, first, what brand do you want?"

There was a broken case on No. 2 hatch and one bottle sitting beside it. She looked at this, and said, "I'll take that stuff. I like the tartan paper the bottles are wrapped in; it's sure cute!"

I did not want to ask her down to the saloon, considering her costume and the grins on the dam' faces of everyone, so we adjourned to the bridge, and in the charthouse she handed me $540, which she took from a bag she had tied round her waist under the kilt arrangement.

"Say, do you mind if the child comes on board and has a run round. She's desperately anxious to see the inside of a ship?"

"Yes, certainly she can come on board. Is she your kiddie?"

"No, she ain't my kid. I'm not married, bo'. Just took her with us. You don't think them ginks near shore will stop a boat with me dressed like this and a kid on board."

I agreed with her that it was a good camouflage. Dick hoisted the kid up. We grabbed her and lifted her to the deck, and she promptly made for the bos'n, who was standing at the entrance to the fo'c'sle, and disappeared under his guidance.

Started handing the 30 cases down to Dick, who packed them forward and spread some old bits of canvas and a fishing net over them.

The chief was standing on the bridge when madam came to him and asked where she could wash her hands. He took her to the W.C. amidships. The waste-pipe there makes a gurgling sound when the ship rolls. She asked, "What's that noise?" The chief answered, "Mice," at which she bolted back to the bridge as hard as she could go.

I gave the kiddie a large cake of chocolate, at which she was delighted, and looked for a bottle of Benedictine to hand to our lady friend, but couldn't find the case. It must have got sneaked over the side somehow or another.

"Well, I hope we shall see you back again," I said as I shook hands with her.

"Sure thing. If this stuff goes well I'll be back. Well, so long;" and she climbed back into her boat, cast off the rope, and away for the shore. We all waved to them, and then looked at one another long and earnestly.

"By gum," the second said, "she had her nerve coming out here in that get up, in among a bunch of men who might have been sober or not."

It was certainly a great surprise, and a very pleasant break in the monotony; we all hope she gets in safely and pays us another visit.

17th June.—I fancy we shall have to move a bit more inshore. The pedlars don't seem to come out so far. A tugboat captain reported to us that there was a lot of firing in the narrows last night and several boats had been caught.

18th June.—Some members of the ship's company had a pretty good night and don't feel quite so good now. We got a boat at 1:30 a.m., which took 30 cases only. One of them that got broken was taken to the saloon, and started the fun. The captain was in his bunk, and Cheery, Doc, mate and second mate were the caste. As far as I can make out (I was on watch and didn't hear the proceedings), the relative value to the Empire of Canada, as represented by the mate, and Australia, as represented by Doc, formed the subject of a discussion which at times got somewhat heated. Anyhow, the meeting broke up in disorder when the Doc tried to kiss the captain, and then went to the chief engineer's room and was told to go to hell when he tried to kiss him. This was at 3 a.m. At four he was contemplating the water from over the taffrail and adding to its density. Started up the engine at two and cruised a bit nearer the shore. At present we still have about 8,000 cases on board. I think last night's attempts at osculation are the result of the lady bootlegger's visit. Served out tots of Board of Trade lime-juice to all hands.

19th June.—This morning I had an old customer who took 30 cases away with him. He says we are in a pretty good position and should do quite well. He told me he was out at a steamer lying about four miles off some nights ago, and all the crew were drunk.

He had bought 25 at $15 and they loaded his boat with 100 and told him to get to hell out of it, which, being a wise man, he promptly did. The crew spent a good part of the day trying to sail wee boats made out of smashed cases. About 6 a.m. the fog came down again, very thick and very hot. Lightning began about 10:30. Then the rain came—so hard that we had to puncture our awning with a knife to let the water out; otherwise it would have burst. Some Frenchmen from a steamer lying near us were laying a long line today and have kindly offered to bring us some fish in the morning if they get a catch. The mate, on the other hand, is proposing that we should help ourselves during the night. The Frenchmen duly kept their promise, and brought a good cod and some ling; they also gave us some small hooks, so that now we are fishing ourselves.

20th June.—The fog is still dense. A boat arrived at 5:30, but wanted non-refillable bottles. This non-refillable fetish is a nuisance. I believe that if you put anything in these bottles it would sell for from $18 to $20.

21st June.—We only got rid of 30 yesterday. Cheery and the mate are at loggerheads. A great number of dragonflies of all sizes and colours appeared on board today. Dick, my black-eyed friend, came off and brought us fresh meat and some cigarettes. I asked him about our lady customer, who, he says, is fine and may be out again soon. He took away 35 cases. Our total for today has been 243, which is not too bad. One boat brought the news that Hamman was coming out with a small schooner for 500, but he didn't turn up. The cutter knocking about without lights, the dirty dog. She pinched one boat and took him in.

22nd June.—Sunday, beautiful day, very hot. Glass high, calm sea. Mate under the influence of gin. We had visitors this afternoon in the shape of the Yankee supercargo and two others off a three-masted topsail schooner lying about a mile off. She had been report-ed to us as having spread the rumour that we were selling doped whisky. When they came on board we quietly surrounded them, took their guns away, and held an impromptu 'court-martial' on the after-hatch. I was president, while captain and Doc acted together as counsel for the prosecution. However, after the court had sat for about half an hour, we came to the conclusion that the accused were innocent. At least, all we could do was to say 'not proven.' They were not at all comfortable during all this. In the end, we handed them back their guns and watched them go off to their own ship. I don't know yet what they came for. Later on in the day the captain and two others off another three-master paid us a visit. The lucky beggars are down to 300 cases. Our first boat came at 8:30 prompt, and left at 8:35 prompt with 30 White Horse. We had a busy night, getting out 301 cases all told. There are a lot of big boats about—one of them a very suspicious fellow, a large white cabin cruiser with a lot of men on board which kept circling round us. Finally she came close, and we allowed one man to come on board, while we kept the rest covered. We are so much lighter now that it is not easy to climb over our gunwales. By his own showing the man had come to negotiate for the cargo, but I imagine he would have had other ideas if he had been less carefully watched. The three-master got his last boat and cleared out about 1:30 a.m.

24th June.—There is a most diabolical type of fly that has just struck the ship, and from all appearances intends to stay with us. It bites like a bulldog, and will penetrate right through tweed trousers. The wee dog went mad today and had to be shot. Cook is inconsolable at losing the pillow for his alcoholic slumbers. The captain tried to kill the dog with a belaying pin, a beastly exhibition. That is the second dog to go mad on board. The first was in Glasgow. Hamman's two boats were out tonight; however, one got the funks and bolted, although the other stayed and took 510 cases. He had an order for over six hundred. The cutter drifted past us with no lights showing, but fortunately did not turn his searchlight on us. No peddling today. The second mate and the mess-boy went swimming. Afterwards they boarded the French steamer practically naked. There is a woman on board of her, but she kept out of the way. While they were on board, the French men caught a shark, so that will put a stop to the bathing.

26th June.—Had a visitor in the shape of the captain of a schooner who wants to buy some whisky. I have offered him 600 cases at $17. He says he will take it and come alongside tomorrow.

We moved to a new position about four miles away. Both of our boats came out this evening. One took the balance of Tuesday's 113 the other one took 500. It looks as though Hamman might stick to his bargain this time. I got a pair of slippers and a pair of khaki trousers, of which I was badly in need, as my clothing is getting pretty well done. I was keeping an emergency pair of trousers on a hook in the bathroom aft. The other day I decided to put them on, and lifted them down, only to discover that there was no seat to them. It had been worn away with the rubbing against the bulkhead caused by our continuous rolling.

28th June.—No boats last night. The rain stopped about midnight. I have had a lot of warnings against piracy and shall have to be on the watch. One boat was caught in the narrows, a fifty-foot boat with twenty men on her, twenty-two rifles, twenty automatic pistols, and sixteen pairs of handcuffs. That wasn't there for nothing. We had visitors to tea, the mate of a two-masted schooner and the supercargo. We have mapped out a golf course on the poop. We play with a rope ring and a T-shaped bit of stick, with circles marked on the deck with chalk for holes. At present I hold the championship with a score of twenty-five for nine holes. The boat that was caught in the narrows tallies in description with the one that was alongside of us the other night, but fortunately we had just finished loading another, so we were all on deck.

29th June.—Sunday, blowing fairly hard all day, and ship rolling so heavily that we can see the round of her bilge when she heels over. Our platform crashed down with the deuce of a rattle of cases in No. 1 hold. I expect some of them will be pretty well smashed up.

30th June.—The Doc has had his first serious case, the chief a job, and the mate a bellyful of someone else's whisky. About 10 a.m. a two masted schooner hailed us and asked for the Doc He boarded her with the mate, and found their engineer lying on a dirty blanket on the floor of the cabin slowly bleeding to death, with a compound and a simple fracture of the left leg. He had been like that for about sixteen hours, poor devil! They had kept him unconscious with brandy! He had slipped into the flywheel pit of the engine, and it's a wonder he wasn't killed. Doc got his leg set and in splints, and with a lot of trouble got him into a speed boat for the shore, by means of a stretcher made of a ladder and a mattress. He came back quite pleased with himself. One of the new destroyers was out today, a four-funnelled fellow doing about thirty to thirty-five knots, with an oil tanker in attendance. If that is a sample of what is coming out tomorrow for good (as we have been told), we are finished. The people on the other ships all say the same. Peddling is done.

PACKING BOTTLES IN SACKS

DINNER IN THE HOT WEATHER

CHAPTER VIII

HIJACKERS

1st July.—There has been a big raid on a ship, a steamer with about 40,000 cases in her. As far as I can make out, it was the one that was selling at fifteen dollars with the crew all drunk. Anyhow, she was raided by forty men, the safe cleared out, and the skipper and super locked up in the charthouse, while the crew were made to work cargo at the pistol-point. They practically cleaned her out in seven days. When they had finished the crew got one hundred dollars each, and all the small schooners round here are full up with stolen booze—Johnnie Walker, White Horse, Black and White, etc. All good brands, which they bought from the raiders as low as seven dollars and eight dollars a case. The wee schooner the chief was in had 800 cases of this whisky. It appears that this ship had no shore connection, and the people here mean to make things nasty for strangers who butt in, which is what would have happened to us had we not all been awake the other night. I don't see much prospect of business as long as these schooners are loaded with stolen whisky which they can sell at eleven and twelve dollars and still make a good profit.

2nd July.—Bos'n has got the shakes again badly and can't get his spoon to his mouth. Evidently he has decided not to eat for the present, as I haven't seen him in the messroom for two days. However, at seven tonight he came to the Doc to see if he could give him anything to buck him up. Doc and I consulted, and we gave him a dose that will keep him mighty busy for the next forty-eight hours, anyway. A boat came at midnight and took 80 cases. I got a letter ashore with him on his promise to deliver it to Hamman first thing tomorrow morning. Previous to that, we were playing 'peever' on the poop, the bad rolling adding a considerable uncertainty to the art of hopping about on one foot. We also had the Highland fling, a sword dance, and sundry other excitements of that nature. Doc was on watch until 12 p.m. I rigged up clockwork on the after-port in the charthouse, and had him running all ways looking to see what was making the noise.

3rd July.—Cheery and the mate engaged in a fierce argument as to whether all gooseberries have hair or not, and nearly came to blows over it. Tomorrow is Independence Day on shore, so I don't suppose there will be any visitors, at least purchasers. There is still a big swell running, which is the reason our boat is not coming out. This blinking mast of ours is getting slacker every day. Another of the backstays has parted, and all the mast wedges at the deck have worked loose and worn through. If it comes down there will be a bonnie mess, as it will probably buckle a few feet above the deck, and how in the name of the 'great mischief' we could ever cut through it without an oxy-acetylene blow-lamp I don't know.

4th July.—Last night nearly had a casualty in the shape of the cook. He had had his usual skinful, and, as there was a fair quantity of stuff to cook, he was staying up. After he had blethered to me on the bridge till I got sick of him, he thought a nap would be useful, and sat down on the galley floor, leant against some lockers, and duly slept. Fortunately, I came down just as he fell over against the front of the range. I just got him away or he would have been badly burned. Captain and mate decorated the ship with the signal flags in honour of Independence Day, and a queer job they made of it. The house-flag was up at the fore crosstrees. I fancy the boss would just about throw a back somersault if he knew, as I don't suppose he approves of Americans since he was chased out of New York.

CHAPTER IX

SQUALLS AND COUNTERFEIT NOTES

5th July.—Got a surprise this morning. At breakfast-time shout of "Aeroplane!" went up. Rushed out of the messroom, and found a sea plane just landing on the water about fifty yards from the ship's side. He signalled for a boat, so we put one out and I went over to him. Captain Ireland, the fellow Hamman told me he sacks once a week, was on board, and said he would take ten cases. So we put the ten in the lifeboat and took them over. Quite a nice wee machine; Ireland says his power is four hundred, but I doubt it. Anyhow, with three men and ten cases it takes him all his time to rise from the water. Judging by our first day's performance, we are going to be busy with this plane. It did four trips: on three of them, just the aviators came out with the cash. They signalled what they wanted and I went over in the boat, gave it to them, and collected the money. It was quite a new experience, counting money in a jumping boat under the wings of a seaplane and handing them whisky in exchange. They take two hours to make the round trip. The day was not to be allowed to pass without additional excitement. At 10:30 p.m. our Newfoundlander decided that he would take the stage, and, mounting the top of No. 2 hatch, just below the bridge, announced unto the heavens and any other interested people that he would have his rights; further, that he didn't know what they were, but, anyhow, he would have the damned things. Judging from his subsequent behaviour it is going to be a long and tedious business getting them, as from his speech on the subject they appear to be mixed up with the sex and attainments of the ship, the amusements of the crew, and the probable destination after death of the chief engineer and Morrison. He further complicated matters by suggesting that the behaviour of the grandparents of most of us had in some mysterious way influenced the matter and that we were morally responsible. Unfortunately, the issue became confused when he and the captain got to grips. Up till then things had been quite amusing, but now they had gone too far, and our extemporary preacher had to be attended to by the mate, who chased him for his life into the fo'c'sle, saying things to him that would take kinks out of a 6 in. chain cable. He then climbed into his bunk and defied the mate to make him go to sleep. After this Morrison was in trouble, came to the chief's room, and drove him into hitting him. As the result, he was carried forward. Then Peters, the managing director of the local laundry, managed to get mixed up in the proceedings and got a cut eye and chin. The chief, usually a most peaceful person, was fairly on the rampage. It's a pity, as I am afraid it will breed bad blood. It's just this infernal lying at anchor that is on everyone's nerves.

6th July.—Had to listen to the evening's battles being fought over again by the contestants, with alcoholic comments by the bos'n, which generally ended up with a shake of the head and the cryptic utterance: "Ah, hum! mph! Well, it's a peetie, mph! hum! To hell with them, anyhow, it's none of my business. I ought to be living aft, but there's no room—mph! To hell with them! Yes, Mac, that's what I say, to hell with them. Ah! mph! Well, it's a peetie!" This went on without any variation except when he called the Almighty as witness to the fact that he had been in his bunk and had had nothing to do with the trouble. Misty and wet. Our aeroplane was out again at midday, and took seven cases this time.

8th July.—Some wild squalls about midday have shifted the wind into the west, so we are lying in the trough and rolling in our very best style. Fresh cabbage for dinner. We still have 6,200 cases on board.

12th July.—It is three months today since we left Bermuda the last time, and we still have 6,000 cases to unload. Everyone is getting darned quarrelsome and liable to go off with a flare at any moment. Mate and captain had a bit of a set to over the bos'n. It was rather funny for all but the participants, especially the bos'n. The mate had had one, and decided he would make the bos'n finish a boat-cover he was working at during his slightly less alcoholic moments. By way of getting it done he promised him, if he would take a big dose of salts from the Doc, to get him a drink from me after. Mr. Bos'n, nothing loath, came aft, and duly took a very aggressive dose of salts. Skipper heard me later in the day getting him some rum, and put his foot down. Poor old bos'n's face when he was told he couldn't get his rum was wonderful. However, it ended by him getting it an hour later, and the boat-cover was duly finished. Mr. Mate then had one himself, and slept it off in the charthouse. A large party went for a sail in one of the boats today, and had to row back about three miles against a nasty wind and sea. The boat won't sail to windward very well.

14th July.—Mate had a good yarn about being dismasted at the Straits of Gibraltar and finding himself a week later within four days' march of Jerusalem wearing a pair of Turkish trousers and a red fez. He didn't explain how he got them or where. His tale was interrupted by a boat who expected to find his pal with an order already here. An hour later two boats came along: one was the pal, the other a big, white, dangerous-looking devil. The pal shouted, "Hijackers," and bolted, so we all got our side arms and prepared for battle. However, the newcomer proved a good fellow, introduced by Lorne, and took 300 White Horse at $17.50. The other two boats that came back later took 300 between them. Loaded the 600 in under two hours.

15th July.—On watch four to eight. Strong north wind blowing. Another four-master arrived, so we are no longer the only pebble on the beach as far as four-masters are concerned. Busy night. Had three boats from Hamman which took over 500 between them. While they were alongside a big white fellow came up; bargained with him and sold him 450 White Horse, making 950 cases for the day.

15th July.—When I counted over the money again by daylight some of the fifty-dollar bills looked funny, and, now that I have compared them with others I have, I am afraid they are spurious—

seven hundred dollars' worth. Showed two to Hamman's people, who said they were dud. If I catch that fellow who planted them on me, I'll beat him up good. I have given Hamman's men a description of him and his boat, and they are going after him; the Lord help him if they get him, for they'll fill him with lead. That crazy lunatic Ireland arrived out with a wee skiff and 15 cases on board that be bad bought elsewhere, and stayed all afternoon with us. He offered me a cheque for five more cases, but I was not having any. Our boats arrived out at about nine—the *Bella*, the *Susai* and a new one. In all they took just on 1,000 cases. A good night's work, and a little later I got rid of 125 dollars' worth of gin. So we are down to 3,400 cases on board.

16th July.—The boat was out early this morning, but he will have to be alongside all day as he daren't go to his landing-place except during darkness. Heard, today that in the last three days over $90,000 of bad notes have been passed out here. One captain took over $11,000 of them, and shot himself yesterday when he discovered it. It appears quite an easy matter to get counterfeit bills ashore; for really good specimens the charge is $15 for a $50 bill and $25 for a $100 bill. About eleven a motor dory came from a three-master and asked for the Doc They have had a petrol fire in their lighting plant—a bad business in which one man has been badly burned. The cook intended sneaking ashore in one of the boats today, and got into his good clothes, but took some gin and went to sleep instead; so he was rather left. The Doc got back at three, and reported a man badly burned from thighs to feet. A boat of ours which was alongside agreed to take him ashore to hospital, so the Doc and second mate went with them to steady the man. Doc got a case of champagne as a fee from the schooner. As the wind has risen and there is a choppy sea, I doubt very much if they will get back tonight. Wrote the boss about the seven hundred dollars I have been done for.

The aeroplane this morning took 17 cases, and he had a job rising from a rough sea. One of our aeroplane lads today gave me rather an interesting and instructive piece of information. He asked me if I had had some bad fifty- dollar bills passed to me. I told him I had. "Well," he said, "so I heard, and, what's more, the guy who told me is mixed up with these hijackers who have an office in Atlantic City, and he said the *Cask* was one of the ships that they had down to raid."

"I think they have been out with that idea twice already," I told him.

"I daresay they have," he said. "You watch out. And don't let anyone know if you have much money on board." I'm glad I got rid of the 39,000 dollars. A large swordfish passed us about nine. I had a shot at him with the rifle, and more or less stunned him, as he went round in circles afterwards. Got the boat out and chased him, but didn't manage a capture: he recovered and went off to keep an engagement elsewhere. He would be about five to six feet long.

17th July.—At 2:30 a very interesting Jersey squall arrived—a regular whirlwind. The water was being licked 25 to 30 ft. into the air. Branches of trees and all sorts of things arrived along with it.

CHAPTER X

THE DOCTOR ASHORE

18th July.—This has been an epoch-making day in the history of Rum Row. I was giving the chief a hand to straighten a shaft on No. 2 winch when I saw a fast white launch coming alongside flying the Coast Guard flag and the Stars and Stripes. There were several men on board and I had the wind up properly, thinking that the Doc must have been caught ashore and they were coming to arrest us. However, as they got nearer I spotted the Doc and second mate on board. The launch came alongside, and our wandering Willies duly climbed aboard. The Doc's story will appear later. Meanwhile, the launch spewed up a naval commander, an army lieutenant, and a Coast Guard captain. The naval wallah is in command of a flying station, while the army lad is in command of a fort near New York. The Coast Guard captain was on duty, but the other two were only joy-riding. This is the first time, I believe, that anyone has been sent back to Rum Row from the shore after being captured; and, what's more, sent back by the U.S. Government in a Government launch, so that's one up for the *Cask*. I invited them down to the cabin and produced 'the cratur,' as they were now on British soil and my guests. We all partook, and waxed merry thereon. The Coast Guard captain gave us some interesting news. He warned us against the *Warrior*, the blighter that did me for the $700; he said they had a bad crowd on board. He also told us he had got a boat smuggling some Italians ashore about ten days ago. He saw it and pursued it, where upon they put the beggars over the side with their hands tied. Eight got drowned, but he managed to pull six out of the water before it was too late. This, he told me, is one way of getting rid of evidence, the punishment for smuggling aliens ashore being at least ten years in a federal jail, while for whisky running it just means the confiscation of the boat and cargo and possibly a hundred dollars fine. The boat is put up for auction the next day, and the owner generally gets it back for a song, as no one bids against him. No wonder the U.S.A. are daily increasing their vigilance out here, when that sort of thing is going on. They stayed about one and a half hours. When they went I gave them a small souvenir to remind them of their visit. They have elected themselves the ship's godfathers, and might prove very useful. The Coast Guard captain has promised to go for the *Warrior* if ever he gets the chance, since tampering with the currency of the country won't do.

Spent the evening listening to the Doc's experiences. He appears to have kept his wits about him and done well. I don't think the second mate would have made as good a job had it been left to him. I must tell the Doc's story as nearly as I can remember it. He has his photograph in several of the New York papers, though I would defy anyone to recognise him from the reproductions.

THE DOCTOR'S STORY

After bringing my fee on board in the shape of the case of champagne and persuading the fellows in the motorboat to take the burnt man ashore, I decided to go and see him put on board and took the second mate to help me. When I got to the *Alice*, I found them trying to make him walk, with his raw, burnt knees, on the deck. I stopped that and had him wrapped in a blanket and carried to the side and lowered into the motorboat. I couldn't get him into the wee cabin, so I laid him under the awning over the well deck, forward of amidships. There was a nasty choppy sea, and, as the man was delirious and struggling, I decided to go ashore and look after him, trusting to luck not to be caught. It was a wet journey. The boat shipped water constantly, and I had a job to keep oilskins over the patient. About halfway in, he came to himself for a bit and complained of cold in his chest; then he relapsed into delirium again. We made into Rockaway and went alongside a jetty. A great number of people came to stare at us and the hurt man. We were pretty objects: second mate in a dirty pair of bell-mouthed white trousers, bare feet, and an equally dirty shirt; I was in no better state, but had shoes on and a sort of tweed deer-stalker hat, evidently a new thing here. I enquired about an ambulance, and was told the nearest civilian one was at least twenty- five minutes off. By this time my patient had become very much worse and I was exceedingly anxious about him; his heart was giving out, being very depressed by the copious doses of brandy he had been given. There was a white motor launch moored not far out, which I found was a Coast Guard launch. I decided to hail him, as he would be able to get the man to hospital much quicker than I could. I did so, and, taking the captain aside explained the situation; he was somewhat astonished, but, placing a guard over us, he went to telephone. Shortly after, down came an ambulance with a doctor and a policeman. I explained things to the doctor, and he got our patient off to the Rockaway Hospital at once. When he had gone my friend the captain informed us that he was very sorry, but we must consider ourselves under arrest, and that we would be taken to the Barge Office in the morning. It was about 9 p.m. by this time. We were put up for the night in a dormitory in the Coast Guard house. I spent a most uneasy night, with the prospect ahead of unpleasant consequences, such as deportation or Ellis Island, or the possibility that the ship might be involved. As condemned men are always supposed to do on the morning of their execution, we made excellent breakfasts, and, as the Coast Guard captain had the 'Clammy Hughie' on us, at his request we got into the launch and started for the 'Battery'—where the Barge Office is—as though we liked it. By this time we had our story cut and dried. It was necessary to clear our friends in the launch of connection with the rum fleet, so we decided to say that we left the *Cask* with our patient in a motor dory—the second engineer in charge— to look for the cutter, with the idea of handing our patient over to her. Not finding her, we hailed this launch near the shore, and persuaded the two fellows, who were fishing, to take us the rest of the way; after which the dory returned to the ship.

On passing the Statue of Liberty it suddenly passed through my mind that we might be searched, so, taking a peep at the captain, who was steering, I started to go slowly through my pockets. I did not wish any document to be found that might cast a bar sinister on my escutcheon or in any way smirch my virgin innocence as far as handling whisky was concerned. I found a small piece of paper in a trouser-pocket, and, on pulling it out, to my horror saw as though in letters of fire:

50 Old Smuggler
100 Uam Var

with the signature of Mr. Mac underneath. That had to be got rid of. With another glance at our captain and guard, I managed to consign this document to the deep, where it soon disappeared astern of us. On arrival at the wharf, we were marched along the streets with two armed guards in rear and a staring populace all round. We were received in silence at first and not even asked for our story. Later, I was requested to 'step this way,' and found myself in a long room containing three desks. At one of these a group of men were gathered—the chief Customs officer and grand inquisitor, his lawyer, two or three Customs officials, a stenographer and the inevitable reporter. This constituted the court of enquiry. I was then put through it for about forty-five minutes. The others seemed to find it interesting, but my interest waned as my desire for the advantages of the open sea waxed.

"Do you know the boss?"
"No"
"Do you know Hamman?"
"No"
"What is the supercargo's name?"
"Must I answer that?"
"Yes"—viciously.
"Then may I consult counsel first?"
"Yes, you may." At that the grand inquisitor sought fresh ground.
"How many cases have you on board?"
"Don't know."
"A thousand?"
"Don't know."
"Two thousand?"

"Maybe."

"Three thousand?"

"Perhaps."

Having assimilated that amount of information, he continued:

"When did you leave Scotland?"

"September."

"Have you any share in the cargo?"

"No."

"Do you receive $40,000 for the trip?"

"No"—most emphatically.

"Do you receive $30,000?"

"No"—just as emphatically.

"Is the stuff paid for on shore or on board?"

"Don't know."

"What is the captain's name?"

I referred to counsel again.

"Do you want to be sent home?"

"No, I want to go back to the ship."

"Do you know I could send you to Ellis Island for a fortnight and then deport you?"

I did not suppose that any answer I might give would improve things, so, like a wise virgin, I kept quiet.

Pulling his face about a bit to make it look fierce, the grand inquisitor started off: "Are you not ashamed of yourself, an educated man, to be breaking the laws of the U.S.A. and trying to smuggle whisky into the United States?" Very fiercely—"You're nothing but a black pirate."

I thought of asking him why a black one, but contented myself with the soft answer that turneth away wrath, by suggesting that I was on board as a medical man and had no interest in whisky; also that, as far as coming ashore was concerned, I should consider myself bound to do the same again to try to save life, and, as far as the ship was concerned, she was not breaking the laws of any State. He evidently considered the answer soft enough, for that ended the inquisition. He then wrote out an order to the captain of the Coast Guard giving us safe conduct back to the *Cask*. Previous to this I had told him I should like to commend the decency of the two men in the motor-launch in helping me. "Yes," he said. "They are good

American citizens, while you are—" And again he referred to my colour and habits.

We were now free, and, after facing numerous cameras, were left to our own devices after having been conveyed back to Rockaway. The mate went for a walk and to find some food, while I stayed and yarned with the captain. I had just bought a clean shirt and a pair of trousers, the breeks to replace the dirty ones of the second mate's. I slept well that night, as I knew we were being sent to the *Cask* again and not to Ellis Island. At 10:30 a.m. we were introduced to the commander of an air station and the captain of a fort,. who were going to come out with us for the trip and for the experience of seeing a bold bad rum-runner at close quarters. I got a sheaf of papers showing myself and describing our adventure, then boarded the launch, and, after an hour's sail, arrived back on board. Very glad I was to feel the shoogly deck of the *Cask* under my feet again, although we were very decently treated by all on shore. The wrath of the chief inquisitor was, I think, two-thirds bluff. Good luck to him for sending us back!

As the launch left us we dipped our ensign, to which compliment she replied with three throaty whoops on a klaxon horn.

CHAPTER XI

NEARLY RAIDED

20th July.—Another Sunday.

21st July.—Captain and second mate were on the war-path early about something or other; at least, I heard second mate calling several people parti-coloured perverters of the truth. He'll get a thick ear all to himself one of these days. The Doc told me today he had heard ashore that the bootleggers have a system of insurance among themselves, and that any man can get a twenty-four hour policy. If no claim is made in that time the policy lapses.

22nd July.—Today we had a new experience in the form of an attempted suicide. It appears that the mate called the cook at 4:30 a.m. for some coffee, rather unnecessarily I think. We all make our own when on watch at night, as cook is, of course, up all day, and had been up till 3:30 trying to bake bread. Anyhow, the monotony of this trip, with the lying at anchor for all these months, and too much gin, have got thoroughly on his nerves. About 7:30 this morning our friend took about fifty pounds' weight of iron rings off our old galley range, tied them round his neck, and proceeded to get overboard. Fortunately someone forward saw him and pulled him back. I first knew of it after breakfast, when the cook came to me crying like a child and said everyone was against him and he would drown himself. Later on in the day cook went for Adams, his versatile assistant, with a carving-knife, because he had hidden his galley rings. His nerves are all to hell, and we will need to watch him or he will go over yet. I did what I could to buck him up.

The wind has risen, and a nasty sea running. No chance of any boats tonight. We have now been 96 days at anchor this trip.

23rd July.—Was awakened by shouting at 5:30 a.m., went on deck, and found that a harbour supervisor's private tug was enquiring the price of whisky. I quoted him eighteen dollars for a small lot, and we slung three cases across to him on a rope. He sent the money in a sea anchor wrapped up in yesterday's newspapers. In one of the papers there was a photo of some of our stuff that was captured the other night on the beach. Very hot all day. Early in the afternoon one of our boats came out with a full crew and stayed with us for the rest of the day, playing poker on the bridge most of the afternoon. I was having a tune on 'Piobmhor' when that weird bird, Captain Ireland, arrived in a small open boat, towing a dinghy. He went off with 50 cases in a craft that no one else would have put thirty in. He's a sportsman. We had a great night's business, getting off in all 1,566 cases in just under four hours. Bos'n had a fine outbreak. I know my playing the bagpipes always rouses his pugnacious instincts; anyhow, he was going to lay out everyone on the ship. However, Peters took an iron belaying pin from him in time, and the rest frog-marched him to his room and tied him up. Then he got loose and stood in the darkness of the fo'c'sle while we were unloading, reviling everyone, and inviting the mate to come to him and he would make love to him in a new way. The invitation was not accepted.

25th July.—Someone on board is getting a taste for brandy. I found a case broached and a couple of bottles missing. For the first time for months the cutter was close alongside us all night. Two hijackers, the *Warrior* and another, a big black devil, were about too. We got ready for action, but the cutter's presence scared them off. I fancy he was acting as our friend and had 'information' that something was coming off. I'm sure the 'godfather business' was working tonight.

26th July.—Early this morning there was a regular naval battle round us. About 5:30 a large speed boat came out from Ambrose, going S.E. like the deuce. The cutter, which was still lying about 100 yards from us, got up steam and went in pursuit, blowing for the speedboat to stop. When no notice was taken the cutter began to fire and blow alternately. The shooting was very poor. I don't think any shot went nearer the target than forty yards. On its way to safety the speedboat had the cheek to stop at two boats for about three minutes each time. One of them was the *Alice*, from which the Doc took the burnt man ashore. After leaving her it made straight out to sea and Soon distanced the cutter. I thought no more about it until, about an hour and a half later, I heard a shot in the distance. Got the glasses and picked up a spot of white foam about two miles away racing towards us with the cutter almost at right angles and coming hard to try to cut him off, firing at the same time. However, the speedboat knew what it was doing, for after it passed us it kept the *Cask* between it and the Revenue boat, so that we were masking the latter's fire. It did the same when it reached the next boat on the line, and kept these tactics up until it was well away inshore. I am sure it must have been doing about thirty knots. Quite an interesting early morning free show while it lasted.

Several things have happened tonight. Firstly, one of our fellows arrived out with an order which I saw had been tampered with, for $25,000 worth of stuff. Off he was packed in double quick time. I am terribly afraid one or two of the other orders are the same; at least, I have been studying them under a strong glass and they look doubtful.

27th July.—Spent most of the forenoon with the Doc and captain studying my last group of orders. The code words are all O.K., but some, I think, are faked, though others appear to be in order. This is the limit, and comes of Lorne not keeping in touch with me and the people who issue the orders ashore when payment is made to them. When the boss was here I at least knew what was doing. Now I can't find out for certain unless I go ashore or Lorne brings me a note of what has been paid in to our office.

Cook was amusing himself again this evening. He managed to get himself 'under the affluence,' so to speak, and got religious cravings, so that he started up the main rigging to look for 'the Almighty' with an axe out of a boat. He reached the crosstrees, and threatened to take a header into the deep or on to a very hard steel deck. It wasn't until the chief engineer told him he had just seen his quarry go into the messroom that he came down. Shortly afterwards he went to sleep in a hold amongst the cases.

28th July.—Decided to look for coal this morning. There is an old gunboat lying about five miles off, so captain, second mate, self and four of the crew started off. It was the peach of a day, oil calm and very hot. We rowed out to the ship in about one and a half hours. They had a very indifferent crowd on board, particularly the officers. The crew are Cubans, all armed, and apparently do just as they please. The chief officer had to consult them before letting us have any coal. We sampled their champagne and got seven bags of coal. They have illness on board of some sort and want the Doc over—in fact, halfway across to them we met their captain rowing over to us to ask for the Rum Row Doc, whom the New York papers have been advertising.

Met Phyllis again today. I don't know if that is her name or not, but she must have one, and that will do as well as anything else. Went back with the Doc and two sailors to the Cuban boat; the Doc departed forward to see a sick sailor, while I yarned with the captain.

Captain Mann wants to get clear of his ship, and has arranged to be paid off on board and hand over to the mate if he can get a passage to Nova Scotia in one of the rum ships going back. He suggested returning with us.

Halfway back to the *Cask* I said to the Doc, "Let's go over to that steamer there, and see if we can buy a ham, or something."

"That's not a bad notion," he replied, and we straightway headed over for her.

They threw us a rope and put over a monkey-ladder. Left a lad on board the boat to keep her off and climbed up on deck. Spoke to the Old Man, who called the steward. I was negotiating with the steward for a couple of hams, when I heard a feminine voice say, "Hub! Mr. Man." I looked round, and coming towards me was our little lady of the bathing costume. She was a vastly different proposition now, and looked damned nice, neatly dressed in dark blue with a white blouse and black tie. Round her waist was a steel chain from which hung a very business-like automatic pistol. We shook hands, and I asked her what she was doing out there.

"Acting as supercargo," she replied, "on behalf of my people ashore, who have first call on all the stuff on board. I'm working with a London guy and am supposed to see he doesn't sell below our figure. Say! I'll be glad to get ashore, boy. It's a rotten job muckin' about here with nix to do half the day."

"I agree with you," I said. "Thank the Lord we are nearly through. I say, do you think you can put in a word for me with that steward? I want two hams."

"Sure. Hey, stooard, this guy here is an old pal of mine; let him have a couple of hams. We can spare them, can't we?"

The steward agreed that the hams could be spared.

"How long are you going to be out here?" I asked the lady.

"Don't know, but I'm hiking for lil' old New Yoik at the earliest possible moment."

The fellow that had the 25,000-dollar order came back tonight in one of the big boats and brought Maloney with him to prove good faith. He also brought a letter purporting to be from the bank, or, rather, from the office that acts as our bank. I suspected another forgery, and told him I had half a mind to stick him down a hold and take him to Nova Scotia with us. At this he looked rather green. However, I talked that over with the captain, and we decided it wouldn't do any good, so after a bit of plain talk we told him he could go back to his boat. The boat tonight had at least fourteen men on board, but we had them covered from the bridge.

Before Maloney left he asked me if I would come ashore with him and satisfy myself. To call their bluff I agreed. They then said they would go over to the *Alice* for some stuff, and come back for me in ten minutes. I got dressed, but three hours after they had not put in an appearance. Two other very large boats had, though, one of them nearly half the size of this one. I fancy they intended to clean out the ship, plus what is in the safe. It has been a near thing tonight; if they had found us busy with Maloney's boat it would have been their opportunity. I am convinced now that Maloney and Co. were in partnership with them.

BARGAINING FOR TEN CASES

AWAY WITH SEVENTEEN CASES

CHAPTER XII

GOODBYE TO RUM ROW

29th July.—Turned in at 2:30 a.m., as there was no sign of
Maloney and Co. coming back. This morning, after a chat with the
captain, with whom I went over the stores and took stock, we found
we had a half-barrel of biscuits, one bag of split peas, a half-sack of
coffee, a half-bag of haricot beans, five 7-lb. tins of mutton; and that
was all. There was very little fresh water left, and we are using the
temporary wood bulkhead between 1 and 2 hatches as firewood for
the galley range. Moreover, since Lorne's last visit we have had no
reliable communication with the shore, and the promised raid will
be managed sooner or later. Taking all these things into considera-
tion the captain and I decided that it was time to quit. We lit up the
donkey-boiler, and had the usual 'hell's broth' of a job getting the
windlass to do its job. Used the last of our coal to get steam. Started
up at 4:30 and went over to the Cuban boat. Got Captain Mann on
board as per my arrangement, and started off on what I intend is
our last trip. Got the balance of the cargo back into the hold—*i.e.*,
943 whisky and 360 gin. Captain Mann told me his owners had
approached Hamman last Saturday to buy 2,000 cases of whisky
from us, as they have nothing but crude alcohol on board, but he
told them it was all sold. Also, he was told that the *Cask* was down
to be 'hijacked' in any case, as they believed there was a lot of
money on board. After balancing my ledger, I found I was only 53
cases out. By midnight we were 45 miles on our way. We have lain
at anchor this trip for 103 stricken days.

31st July.—Dull and cloudy all day. We are heading across the St.

George's shoals. I hope we get no strong S.E. winds, for the swell breaks to the bottom over an area of about twenty square miles. We passed through several schools of porpoise, and I had a shot at some of them. Weather looked very dirty for a bit about 10 p.m., with a lot of lightning to the S.E. Signed on Captain Mann as pilot.

1st August.—Beautiful morning. Went through a school of about seventeen whales. They were diving under the ship. Got another surprise this afternoon. We saw a trawler about eight or nine miles to the S.E., which, on sighting us, altered course to intercept us. At first we thought he had been fishing, and were looking forward to exchanging some whisky for fresh fish. Hard biscuits, peas, and haricot beans may be sustaining, but as an exclusive diet they pall very quickly. However, when we were close to him he signalled he wanted to speak. Captain Mann, who knew the skipper, went over in the mate's peculiar dinghy to buy whatever he could. He came back with a bag of potatoes, a small sack of flour, 16 lbs. of fresh meat, 6 tins of milk, some cigarettes and—to my astonishment—a letter from the boss. The letter read:

> 'DEAR CAPTAIN,—Immediately on receipt of this get up anchor and come to Halifax at once, irrespective of what number of cases you have on board.'

He must have got wind of something serious. The trawler was the *Utopia*, and is on her way to New York, with instructions to deliver this letter to us in passing.

3rd August.—Mate came to me about 7 p.m. and said, "Look here, Mr. Mac, if we are not in in time to be passed by the doctor, we shall have to anchor below the entrance to the harbour. If we do, how are we to get that blasted anchor up again now that our coal is finished?"

"I don't know," I said. "What time does the doctor go off duty?"

"About eight, I think, and I don't see us getting in before 9:30."

"Well, what about taking the pilot below and having a smoking concert, while we just go straight in and drop anchor in the middle of the harbour."

Off went the mate, and presently the pilot, who was a dashed nice chap, arrived aft and joined Doc and myself.

4th August.—About 6:30 the following morning I awoke to find the pilot lad standing at the entrance to the saloon and doing his best to fix a small, made-up bow tie to the stud at the back of his neck. In due course the Customs arrived, along with the doctor. Gave them my list of cargo, etc., and they sealed up the hatches.

Got all my papers and cash (about £5,000) into a suitcase and went ashore to meet the boss, wondering very much if any of the orders had been tampered with. Met the boss at his hotel, and we immediately compared the orders with a list of amounts paid into the office in New York. As I feared, some of the orders had been faked up, but I must say he took it very well indeed.

"I expected something of this sort," he told me, "after I got a letter about a fortnight ago from Stalman, a friend of mine, who has gone into partnership with a man who knows Hamman. He told me Hamman & Co. were up to some monkey tricks with our orders, and that already three attempts had been made to raid the ship. Is that the case?"

I explained what had taken place.

"When that letter came to me from Stalman," he went on, "I decided you had better come here with the money and the cargo, rather than lie there any longer and lose the lot. Hence my order to the captain to move at once. The thing is done and can't be helped, but, if Lorne had only carried out my instructions to him and kept in touch with you and the office, they could have got away with no more than one. In any case, we're not going to go bankrupt."

"Who are the ship's agents here?" I asked; and he told me. "I must get food out for dinner. Do you know, we are down to a few biscuits, peas, beans and a little coffee?"

"Right," he said, "off you go, and we'll discuss the whole thing fully later on."

When I reached one of the wharves and was looking for a boat to take me out, a gentleman in blue with a lot of gold on his cap came up to me and asked, "Are you in charge of that bald-headed four-master out there?"

"No, not exactly, but I have something to do with her. Why?"

"Why?" he said. "It's not why only. It's why the hell you are lying there instead of being below the island?"

"I don't know, I'm sure," I said. "We just came in last night and anchored."

"There's something funny about this," he went on, "for the pilot says he anchored you below the island. I admit the man's not very well and may be mistaken, but, whether he is or not, you've got to shift."

It then occurred to me to ask him who be was. "Who am I, my friend? I'm the harbour-master, and you must shift at once."

"I'm sorry, but we can't shift, for there is no coal on board to raise steam with, and we can't get the anchor up. If you send us out coal we'll move."

"I'll send you no coal and you've got to get to blazes out of there by six o'clock tomorrow morning and go straight over to the far side."

"Why?" I asked. "We aren't near any other ships ; there's plenty of sea room."

"Well, if you must know, you are exactly where I have arranged that the *Hood* shall lie when she gets here tomorrow."

I burst out laughing, much to the harbour-master's annoyance. To think of the old *Cask* trying to have a tilt at the mightiest battle-ship of the British Navy, indeed of any navy—just like her blasted cheek! It was finally arranged that a tug would attend to us later on.

I was on board when the tug came out, put the bight of a wire hawser round our cable, and steamed slow ahead until it tripped the anchor; then lifted it with a winch and towed us well out of harm's way.

Had a fine hot bath when I got back to the hotel. I also saw the boss, who said he had written Lorne a month ago to tell me to watch Hamman's men very carefully. But Lorne had given the letter to one of them to hand to me instead of bringing it himself. I suppose the man simply tore it up.

5th August.—The crew are all anxious about bonuses, and are asking me if they are to get them. I don't think boss intends paying any, so I am non-committal. Some of them don't deserve any, but there are others that do. I'll fix what I can for them. *Hood, Repulse* and *Adelaide* came in this morning about ten.

The boss has refused to pay a bonus and there's a rare racket on board. I think they will go to court. The mate tried to get some bottles off, but didn't succeed, as the Customs man who lives on board knows him of old and keeps a gimlet eye on him.

CHAPTER XIII

LAWSUITS AND LEAVE-TAKINGS

6th August.—As Captain Mann thinks he can sell the balance of our cargo, I have told him to go ahead and try. A very important lad arrived this morning with a sheaf of papers, which he proceeded to paste on to the main mast. This was a peculiar proceeding, so I went and asked him what the devil he thought he was playing at?

"I'm a sheriff officer," he told me, "and this vessel is arrested until the matter set forth in these documents is settled."

I read the documents, from which it appeared that the captain and most of the crew have been to a lawyer about bonuses, with this result. The poor old *Cask* is now in jail!

From where we are lying it's quite easy to see the terrible effect of the explosion that took place here during the war. About half the town must have been laid flat. Doc and self had a thorough exploration of the place tonight under Captain Mann's able guidance, and managed to amuse ourselves quite satisfactorily. Anyhow, we had a dashed good supper. Doc is anxious to get back to England, and I am trying to get him off via Montreal. Boss told me today he was trying to get a load of pulp for home, but the authorities won't let the ship go up the coast to another port to load it as long as there is whisky on board. There is nearly as much smuggling going on here as off Long Island.

9th August.—We are paying off all of the crew that don't live on the Eastern fringe of the Atlantic. As these are the lads who are making the case and have refused to sign off, I paid their wages into the shipping office. The boss has deposited the amount of their claim into court, so that the *Cash* may return home as soon as possible. So the documents are now off the mainmast.

Mann told me today that he had two men who are willing to put up 13,000 dollars between them to take the balance of our cargo. We could transfer it to them at sea, but the cash has to be deposited in a bank here first.

15th August.—The case of crew versus *Cask* comes up tomorrow before the Admiralty Court. I have been subpoenaed as a witness and am not looking forward to it.

We have got a new captain and mate and three deck-hands signed on. The mate is a Dutchman and holds an extra master's certificate. That's the first time since the end of November that there has been a certificate on board: if it counts for anything, we should have a record run home.

We have arranged that our fellows shall get a bonus when we pay off in Glasgow. The Mann deal is off, as his friends can't raise the necessary cash.

6th August.—Went to the court at 10 a.m. The bos'n, Morrison and Peters had also been summoned, but did not put in an appearance, so were 'attached' and sent for while we adjourned for an hour. Judge gave them a rating, after which their evidence was taken. The court adjourned again till eleven on Monday morning. Got the Doc off via Montreal. Peters, Morrison and Co. have withdrawn their claim, much to the others' annoyance. Our cook has gone back to Bermuda with something in his pocket, so he is out of it also.

At midday today we got the *Cask* down to the oil quay. We couldn't get proper oil, so only took five tons to mix with what is still on board. That gives them about eighteen days' steaming, so they will have to be careful. Went so far with her, and then got into the Customs launch that had accompanied us. We started back, while I sat in the stern watching the *Cask* getting smaller and smaller and wondering what mischief she would be up to on her trip across. She has been my home for a year all but a fortnight, and if it had not been for this court case I would have been still on board. Smuggled three bottles of whisky ashore on the Customs launch.

18th August.—Went to the court again at eleven. We were five minutes late. All the witnesses were cleared out, so I went to sleep in the banisters' room till one, when we adjourned till 2:30 p.m. There was a chance I might not be called, because neither side knew what I might say and they were both scared. So it happened, and I spent the whole blessed afternoon in the barristers' room. Judgment will be given on Friday, but, as we won't be here, the agents will deal with the matter.

19th August.—We leave today at 4:30. Got my discharge marked 'V.G.' at the shipping office, otherwise I would have had a job getting into Britain. I think we sail by the *Carmania* on Friday from Quebec. I expect the immigration authorities will be after me. I applied there for their special pink form, but couldn't get it without producing a ticket, which I hadn't got, showing I was leaving Canada. I'm not going to bother. Packed up and caught my train, which is most comfortable.

20th August.—Arrived at Quebec at 2:30. Booked our passages by the *Carmania*, which sails at 4:30 p.m. tomorrow, the 21st August.

EPILOGUE

HERE we are, two days out from Quebec, and, curiously enough, I am beginning to regret that the *Cask* had to sail without me. Possibly distance lends enchantment to the view, but I don't know. There is a fascination in being close to the sea in all her moods, and in a great ship like the *Carmania* the sea is far away. It is no longer intimate; a squall or a big wave has no influence worth mentioning. Standing below the bridge, looking forward, it seems inevitable that in five days and ten hours, to a moment or so, we shall be safely alongside a Liverpool wharf. No one wonders if tomorrow will see us fifty miles to leeward of our course or battling up to make a port that was within sight the day before yesterday. The mystery of tomorrow is gone, the lure that takes us off the beaten track. Tomorrow I know that I shall breakfast at eight, have soup at eleven, lunch at one, and play deck skittles from three to four. It is a tame prospect. Yes, I do regret the old *Cask*, with her glorious (though at times damnable) uncertainties, and particularly I regret the company of those who stuck by her all along and of the new-comers who stayed with us when the real business of the trip began: the old Cap with his 'don't-care-a-damn' attitude to broken pars and rent sails; the Doc with his quaint ways; the chief, who was always willing and always working away at something; the second, with his inevitable joke; the old bos'n who, despite his eternal thirst, could stitch a sail, or make one, with the best; the laundry firm of Morrison and Peters, with whom I spent many a stormy watch off the coast; our first stowaway, whom we made cabin-boy and who was always in some 'pother;' and, last but not least, Ping Pong our donkey-man, who would do anything for me at any time, and never grumbled. Those are the fellows from whom I parted with real regret, for without their loyalty our enterprise would have been a hopeless fiasco.

Even if I haven't made my fortune, it has been well worthwhile to spend a year learning something about those who go down to the sea in ships, what manner of men they are and what blue water can be like. Naked nature though it was, it was good. So, when I am again sailing a wee motorboat on the Clyde, or a lug-sail in the West Highlands of Scotland, I'll think of the days when I had something to do with the adventure of 'what will tomorrow bring' on board the schooner *Cask*.

- END -

PUBLISHER'S AFTERWORD

As with many accounts of Prohibition, the exact names and descriptions of people and places in this narrative were changed so as not to incriminate the guilty—particularly so in cases when Prohibition was still the law of the land. *The Diary of a Rum-Runner* was published in Great Britain in 1929 and in the United States in 1930. Prohibition wasn't repealed until December 5, 1933.

As full of facts as his narrative is, the author of *The Diary of a Rum-Runner* apparently succeeded in concealing his identity. The editors have not been able to document him, so it is likely that the name Alastair Moray was a pseudonym, for it was said no one used their real name while on Rum Row. When one of Moray's fellow countrymen, Eric Sherbrooke Walker, wrote of his smuggling experiences in *The Confessions of a Rum-Runner*, published in 1928, he used the pen name James Barbican. But while Walker, or Barbican, was actively engaged in rum-running while on U.S. soil—and was even under indictment for conspiracy to violate the National Prohibition Act—Moray never entered U.S. waters or broke U.S. laws.

It is evident that the name of Moray's ship, the *Cask*, was changed in his account. According to sighting reports from the U.S. Coast Guard cutter *Manhattan*, a British schooner named *Rask* was on Rum Row 13 miles off New York on or around June 23, 1924. This time period and location correspond to Moray's diary.

Lloyd's Register of Shipping lists the *Rask* as a 187-foot, four-masted, steel auxiliary schooner with tonnage similar to what Moray claimed. Built in 1915 in Aalborg, Denmark, for the timber trade, the *Rask* was named for one of her owners. Around 1923 her port of registry was changed from Haugesund, Norway, to London. The new owner was R. G. Fothergill.

It was, and still is, a seafaring tradition for sailors to assign nicknames to their ships. *Rask* to *Cask* is no great stretch, but was a clever fit for the line of work they were engaged in. *Cask* was certainly a better name for use in a book by a rum-runner, and in no way would its use besmirch the good Danish name of her former owner. The *Rask* became a well-known figure on Rum Row, as newspapers were quick to point out. On March 7, 1924, the *New York Times* reported that the liquor fleet lying about 12 miles off the approaches to New York City had increased to 28 vessels—the most since Christmas 1923. Federal scouts told reporters they heard strains of jazz and sounds of song and laughter. Of the vessels, the *Rask* was sighted off Montauk, the eastern tip of Long Island.

In May 1924 writer James C. Young spent a week aboard the Coast Guard cutter *Seminole* on rum patrol duty. He described what he saw and heard as a witness of practical Prohibition enforcement on the high seas for the *New York Times*: "Next in order we visit the *Rask*, with London prominently painted on her bow. The *Rask*'s crew is friendly and turns out in force to grin and wave. It is washday and the rigging flaunts an odd assortment of male tackle. But one piece of attire pinned there never belonged to any man aboard. This is a little girl's dress, a tiny little girl about 2 years old. It is blue and pretty and hangs bravely from a ratline, taking the morning air. Whose little dress is this?"

In mid-July 1924, Moray's shipmate "Doc" received national recognition following his act of mercy in entering U.S. waters to save the life of one of a fellow rum-runner's crew. Newspapers all around the country picked up his story with great zeal and dubbed him the "Rum Row Doc."

With his real name listed as Ralph Folkes (sometimes Roystan Foulkes), Doc told U.S. authorities that he was a native of Sydney, Australia, and a graduate of universities in Glasgow and London. He left school in June 1923 because his funds ran out. Seeking employment, he shipped as the medical officer aboard the Rask for a three-month voyage to Bermuda. He explained that without a diploma he could not practice medicine and that the position would give him the experience he sought. He also said he wanted adventure and material for writing fiction.

Articles further stated that Doc's patient was Ralph Conrad of Loungsberg, Nova Scotia, who had contracted pneumonia and appeared likely to die if he were not taken to a hospital. During his emergency passage, Doc was accompanied by Philip Smith, a mate from the *Rask*. The *Washington Post* summed up Doc's adventure, stating: "The doctor, whose practice is confined to the offshore whisky armada, was arrested by immigration authorities for having landed on American soil without a passport. When it was learned his mission was one of mercy, undertaken in behalf of a sailor near death, he was sent back to the rum fleet in a Coast Guard cutter, with a special escort and under a white flag."

The *Rask* made headlines again at the end of July 1924 when two letters from a Rask crewman were found on the person of a rum-runner—the same runner who had ferried Doc ashore the week prior—who was captured by the Coast Guard on the way in with a load obtained from the *Rask*. One of the letters did not have a stamp and was opened. Written by crewman Robert W. Wylie Jr. and addressed to his father at Glasgow, Scotland, it read:

> Just a line to let you know all is well and dandy. Don't write any more as we are nearly empty and shall soon be home. We are having fine weather and have only about 2,000 cases, which we will discharge in two days if all goes well. I hope you and the family are all right as this finds me well, and if I get all my bonus and the wages due me I'll not forget to bring some presents home.
>
> There are so many sales here and things are four times cheaper than at home. Well, parents, this is a very exciting life out here. There are two boatloads of Chinese, Italians, Greeks &c., all waiting to be smuggled into the States. There are also a couple of steamships with opium, heroin, morphine and cocaine, all of which is being smuggled in every day.
>
> There is a seaplane that comes out and loads nineteen cases which it carries on each trip, making over six trips

daily. There is a launch near by and I must close. With love and kisses to all.

Newspaper editorialists expressed outrage and used the text of the letter as proof of the claim that Prohibition was actually aiding the smuggling of aliens and narcotics.

The rest of Moray's account fully checks out. The Coast Guard cutters he encountered correspond to Coast Guard records; ocean liners he sighted are confirmed by transit schedules; and, the names of other vessels he spotted can be corroborated by sighting reports and newspaper stories. Surely, the strongest evidence that Moray's account is wholly accurate is the set of photographs he personally took on Rum Row.

Finally, two additional observations Moray noted in his diary serve to tie Moray to other well-known rum-runners and Rum Row episodes. First, in his July 1 entry, Alastair Moray makes note of a hijacking but does not mention the name of the vessel. This was actually one of the largest hijackings to take place on Rum Row, and the most thrilling for newspapers to follow. On June 24, 1924, the French steamer *Mulhouse* was boarded by 20 raiders, her crew were held hostage for ten days, and 35,000 cases were sold over the side at deep discounts to the other rum-runners. The *Mulhouse* affair, as it became known, made headlines and stayed in the news for years. Finally, in 1928 a French court declared that the ship was on the high seas when pirated and that insurance on the cargo, admittedly destined for American consumption and valued at a half-million dollars, must be paid.

Just a few days earlier in June 1924, the *Mulhouse* was on the sighting report of the Coast Guard cutter *Manhattan*, along with 22 other rum-running steamers, schooners, and barkentines. Along with the *Rask* was the *M.M. Gardner*, a British-flagged schooner owned by William F. McCoy. McCoy, whose fair-dealing and quality liquor perpetuated the phrase, "it's the real McCoy," had been captured by the Coast Guard a few months prior and was awaiting trial. In his book, *The Real McCoy*, McCoy wrote that he was wrongfully accused by the owners of the *Mulhouse* of masterminding the hijacking. The *M.M. Gardner* did, however, purchase some of the discounted liquor and sell it over the side.

Before selling the cargo to fellow rum-runners, the pirates offered Captain Christopher Benham of the U.S. Coast Guard Station at Townsends Inlet, New Jersey, $2 a case to "turn his back." Captain Benham declined the $70,000 bribe and later told the *New York Times* that he would rather be poor all his life than violate his oath as an officer.

Moray frequently mentions the rum running mother ship *Star*, a Rum Row competitor. Under her real name, *Istar*, this grand steam yacht was often called the "Queen of Rum Row" or the "Aristocrat of Rum Row." James Barbican wrote about her under a fictitious name in his *The Confessions of a Rum-Runner*.

Built in Scotland in 1897, the 319-foot *Istar* was the former yacht *Nahma*, which belonged to the Goelet family, whose wealth was derived from New York banking and real estate. The yacht served in the U.S. Navy in World War I as the USS *Nahma II*. Ironically, the "Queen of Rum Row" was a semi-sister ship to the USS *Mayflower*, the presidential yacht used during Prohibition by Warren Harding and Calvin Coolidge.